ME AND MY

Why Women Stalk Other Women
When An Unhealthy Curiosity becomes
An Unstoppable Obsession

Written by Kimberley Alice

While every precaution has been taken in
the preparation of this book, the publisher
assumes no responsibility for errors or
omissions, or for damages resulting from the
use of the information contained herein.

Me And My Shadow: Why Women Stalk Other Women

When An Unhealthy Curiosity becomes
An Unstoppable Obsession

First Edition. July 06, 2024.

INTRODUCTION

Stalking! Not your everyday occurrence for most people, but if you are unlucky enough to be one of the chosen few who seem to have picked yourself up a little bit of an obsessional stalker, then this book is for you.

In these pages, I tell my story of being stalked for many years by a rather nasty, vindictive female stalker. I outline the traits of women who stalk other women and lay bare the reasons behind their actions. I also delve into the profound effects stalking has on its victims and what you can do to protect yourself from emotional and psychological harm.

For some victims, the experience is short-lived, but for others, it can continue for many years. My obsessional stalker launched an online stalking and harassment campaign, using modern technology to threaten and intimidate. This book chronicles how I countered my stalker's every move and ultimately turned the tables, putting a stop to the harassment through the use of reverse psychology tactics.

This isn't just a story of survival but a guide to understanding and countering the mind games played by stalkers. My journey is filled with lessons on resilience, resourcefulness, and the strength found within the depths of fear and intimidation.

Whether you are currently dealing with a stalker, know someone who is, or are simply curious about the dark world of stalking, my story will provide you with insights, strategies, and a sense of solidarity. You are not alone, and with the right knowledge and tactics, you can reclaim your life.

Welcome to my journey, and may it empower you to find your strength and voice against those who seek to cause you harm.

CHAPTER ONE

What Has Stalking Got to Do with Me

So glad you asked, my stalking trauma began in the summer of 2022, we were half way through June of that year, I was sitting in my camper van in Poole Harbour watching paddle boarders paddling on the calm waters, it was a lovely day, the sun was shining and I had just got engaged, my fiancé was sitting next to me and we were just sitting peacefully looking out of the side door of the camper across the harbour watching lots of boats bobbing on the surface of the water with the glint of the sun sparkling like diamonds.

I placed our engagement rings on the bottom of an upturned rainbow coloured wine glass and stood it next to a bottle of bubbly that we were planning on opening later that evening on the beach after the sun had gone down, I took a photo on my mobile of our rings with the harbour in the background against a perfect blue sky, we both looked at the photo and agreed that it was lovely, so I uploaded it to my social media accounts marked as friends only announcing our engagement and thought nothing more of it.

We watched to sun going down the sky was a wonderful deep orange, like the sky was on fire, I took a few more photos and posted them up too, once the sun had gone down and it was dark, we moved from Poole harbour over to Bournemouth beach, we found a lovely little spot to park the camper van to stay overnight and took our wine glasses and bottle of champagne down to the beach.

We found a nice spot on the beach not too far away from some night fishermen and we sat down on the soft sand, we had bought a little tin bucket with us to start a small, controlled fire while we drank our champagne. Once we had our little fire going and we had poured the champagne into our glasses, we took our engagement rings out of our pockets and opened the little boxes that they were sitting in, I removed my fiancés ring from his box and placed it on his ring finger and he did the same for my ring, we both looked at each other smiled and kissed, then we sat drinking our champagne while the flames of the fire flickered in the darkness, we could hear the waves lapping on the beach and right at that moment in time nothing else mattered to us.

We just sat for a few hours listening to the sound of the waves and watching the night fishermen, breathing in the smell of the fresh sea air, with the gentle breeze on our faces, just idly chatting about nothing in particular. We packed up about 2am and headed back to the camper van to settle down for the night.

We woke up early and took a slow walk along the beach, we grabbed an ice cream before heading back home.

Fast forward to today, I have been stalked for so long now that I cannot remember how life was prior to when my experience with a stalker began, my life went from living a purely innocent existence to one of having to hide my identity in all places known to man.

Hell, really hath no fury like a woman scorned.

My life prior to picking up a rather nasty vindictive stalker was one of not having to second think my every movement, I was emotionally and physically free to do as I pleased, there were no corners of the earth that were not available to my exploration, I could meet up with friends and drive my car anywhere that I wanted to go at any given time. My life was happy and carefree, I held healthy relationships with all my family and all my friends, and I enjoyed going to work, I had the normal day to day worries that everyone has, I was in a happy place.

Oh, to travel back to these happier times, I would give anything to have a time machine, to be able to just zip back for a few moments of rest and peacefulness, somewhere I could just sit with my soul quietly and be at one with my surroundings with no feelings of danger of personal threat at all.

Before being stalked and harassed I took this peaceful existence for granted, right up until the time it was ripped away from me, and my emotional trauma began.

Stalking is an age-old obsession that has grown into a very large problem in modern times. When you think of a stalker your mind automatically generates this dark sinister vision of a male figure trying to hide his face with a large hat wearing very dark glasses and an oversized beige raincoat, but that is not the typical look of a stalker today, it is very different.

Modern day stalkers can gain information on others and cause mental and psychological harm to their victims without ever having to leave the safety of their own home, anyone with access to the internet and mobile technology can stalk a person from anywhere in the country or even anywhere in the world, there are no boundaries when it comes to stalking in today's times, due to the advances in technology a stalker no longer needs to stand outside a persons' house or visit their work location to gain personal information on them, they don't need to get physically close to their victims because the internet has removed all social and personal barriers and enabled a stalker to get up close and personal from miles away!

Years ago, it was harder for a person to stalk, there were no social media accounts that a stalker could troll through, mobile technology is the modern-day curse if it falls into the wrong hands, and you need to be tech savvy and hold a degree in technology to be able to use it to adequately enough to be able to protect yourself from cyber stalking and harassment.

Mobile phones have evolved into smart technology in a handheld device, mobile phones have come a long way since the first "brick phones" that were huge and you had to carry the small suitcase sized battery with it, my dad had one of the first phones issued to him, it was the DynaTAC 8000x made by a Motorola employee named Martin Cooper, the year was 1983. My dad was like the cat that got the cream when he came home carrying that in, the smile he was wearing covered the whole of his face he was chuffed to bits, this new technology he was holding in his hand that not many people had access too, roll forward to today and practically everyone owns a mobile phone.

The DynaTAC 8000x didn't come with inbuilt systems that enabled you to call, text and email a person, you couldn't browse the internet and do all your shopping with it, it was just a phone to voice call people on, now jump forward 20 years to today, with all the mobile technologies we take for granted. It's a massive technology leap in capabilities. The original intention behind all these advancements was to make peoples' lives easier, to reduce the gaps in communication and make things faster and more efficient, but in the wrong hands, as always, this kind of technology is always used to do everything it was "not" intended to be used for.

When we are inventing new things, the inventors are not thinking of the sinister ways in which their inventions can be used, they are focusing solely on the positives and all the good ways their inventions can help people and improve their lives, but there are always those people who will use any invention for their insidious desires to cause mayhem and stir up drama and exploit the systems that were invented for good uses.

With technology becoming smaller and lighter and most people now having access to mobile devices and the internet it has made it possible for so many people to use technology in a very nasty way, hate crimes are increasing, we are seeking more online stalking and harassment cases every day.

With the advances in technology most things are smaller and lighter, the capabilities have been enhanced tenfold, TVs are smaller with inbuilt smart technology that enables you to download and stream films directly from the internet onto both your tv and your mobile phones.

Personally, I love all these advancements, I love technology, I work in the IT business, I have used tech to make my life easier, I have designed websites and built platforms for advertising and selling on, my hobby is photography, I designed my own website and hosted it myself, I used all my own photographs so there was no chance of breaching any data protection and copyright laws at all.

I love it when I can work on a manuscript on my home pc and upload it to my one drive, then if I am out and about somewhere and think of something more to add to it, I can log into my home pc using my mobile and add what I need then hit save, it's great that when I arrive home later I can log on again and carry on from where I left off with all the extra bits I added when I was on the move. Brilliant!

I can access my emails on the go, well, only if my stalker isn't having a narcissistic rage episode and continually locking my account by inputting multiple failed account log on attempts that is!

Over the years my stalker has used technology in so many ways to try to hurt me and cause me psychological, emotional and reputational harm, she has displayed this uncanny ability to pop up causing a menace of herself right at the most inconvenient time, credit where it is due, I have to say, her timing was always impeccable, she would appear out of the blue like the Green Witch in the Wizard of Oz bringing along with her, her septic nature to spoil my entire day.

Where did I pick my stalker up from, I hear you ask, roll back to me getting engaged and posting a nice photo of our rings on my social media! It all started right there! That one simple photo I posted of our beautiful rings, a joyous moment that we both wanted to share with our family and friends, it's not every day that you get engaged and we innocently posted our happy occasion so that the people closest to us could join in with our celebrations of our happy life event.

Not everyone was happy for us that day
when we announced our news!

My fiancé, who is now my husband, his exe girlfriend was not happy at all, she had refused to accept that their relationship had been over since before Christmas the previous year, he had moved out of their address they shared together and informed her that he had no intention of ever returning. They had been having relationship issues for the last two years leading up to them permanently separating. His exe girlfriend knew he wasn't happy at all, she had felt him starting to break away and she was trying to keep reeling him back in, he had left her several times over the last few years of their relationship and stayed at a friends' house or gone back to living at his parents' house for a while, but she had always managed to talk him into going back with promises of her changing her behaviour and not being so controlling and nasty to him, for the first few days she would be different but within a short time of him returning she would always revert back to her awful behaviours, and after years of this repeating pattern he finally plucked up the courage and left her for good.

She spent the next 10 months hounding him with thousands of messages, asking why he had broken up with her, and trying to get him to see that in her eyes he was the problem never her. She spent months accusing him of being violent and aggressive towards her, but all I ever witnessed in all that time was how abusive she was in her treatment of him, I never saw any evidence of him behaving in the way she was accusing him of behaving towards her, in fact it was the total opposite, it was her who was being manipulative and controlling, she was the abusive person and every time he asked her to stop being abusive she immediately denied being abusive at all.

The more he tried to reason with her, the more unreasonable she became, what she was saying wasn't making any sense to him at all nor anyone else who read any of her messages. Her mindset was not a healthy one, she was not only unreasonable, but she was totally delusional too, and it made trying to hold mature conversations with her just impossible, any conversations were of the abusive kind, there was never any closure or resolution to whatever it was that she was screaming at him about either, their heated discussions just went round in never ending circles.

From January right up until June when she discovered our engagement, she just kept bombarding him with hundreds of messages a day every single day.

When I asked him why he didn't just block her, his answer was always the same, if he blocked her then she would come looking for him and make his life even worse. He told me it was better that she could contact him, otherwise it would annoy her even more and she would get out of hand, he even tried approaching her mother to ask if she could talk to her daughter and get her to calm down enough so he could hold a conversation with her long enough to reason with her, but once her mother his exe know that she had been contacted it made her worse, she started threatening him and told him not to talk to anyone else about her ever again, she threatened him saying if he did talk to anyone about her she would hurt him and make his life a misery, she didn't say it as politely as I have written it, her language was foul and abusive with lots of swear words too.

He was living in fear of her daily, he was absolutely terrified of her, constantly worried about what she would do to him or what she would say, he lived in fear of her turning up where he was.

When we met, he weighed in at just under 7 stone! He was so skeletal and obviously highly anxious that he couldn't function properly at all, he wasn't eating properly nor was he sleeping well either, he still doesn't to this day. The years he had suffered in silence due to the appalling behaviour of his exe girlfriend had taken its toll on him. He was medically diagnosed as suffering with general anxiety disorder, he had "at risk of domestic abuse and domestic violence" written on his medical notes, he was later confirmed as suffering with complex post-traumatic stress disorder (C-PTSD) and to add to it all he didn't leave our house for over a year, the only time he left the house was to go to work and come straight back again.

He disclosed to me that during their time together she had regularly used emotional blackmail tactics to manipulate and control him, she would belittle him and berate him and blame him for her being a failure, she constantly deflected all her insecurities onto him, she never took responsibility for her words nor her actions, and she always had an excuse for behaving how she did towards him by turning it around on him saying it was him that made her angry and because of him she started throwing things and breaking things.

9

She threw him out of the house once and messaged him saying all his personal belongings were thrown out on the front lawn and all his expensive tools were sitting there too, she told him to hurry up and collect them before someone stole them, then she went from being abusive and extremely aggressive to hysterically laughing at him and ridiculing him. This abusive behaviour became their normal routine right up until the day he left and swore he was never going back to her.

He was caught in what is known as an abuse cycle and her found it extremely difficult to break this ongoing cycle and leave. An abuse cycle is a four-stage pattern used to describe the way abuse often occurs, the stages are tension, incident, reconciliation and calm, this is repeated in abusive relationships, and sometimes it can be difficult to spot that this is happening to you, but eventually you start to see the patterns forming and you begin to recognize that this is happening to you.

During his relationship his self-esteem had been eroded to a point where he was being kept in a constant state of panic, anxiety and fear, one example of the emotional trauma he endured happened when she just took off in his van and she went missing for three days, with no sign of her, and no sign of his van at all, she turned her mobile phone off so he was not able to contact her at all, he became so panicked he tried contacting her friends to see if she was ok, eventually he contacted her mum who phoned the police, the police confirmed a sighting of his van had been made driving towards another town, the town his van was sighted in by the police was his exe girlfriends home town, so the assumption was made that she had gone to visit friends, the police gave him a reference number and told him that if she hadn't come home by the end of the weekend to phone them and report her as a missing person, he was informed that the police could not class her as missing until 48 hours had elapsed.

Her young son from a previous relationship was living permanently with her mother because of her volatile nature when she had just totally vanished with no word of where she was and no way of contacting her, she returned three days later, all hyper and slurring her words, it was clear she was either intoxicated or high on some kind of substance. She acted like nothing had happened and blamed everyone for overreacting, she made no mention of where she had been and got violent and aggressive when questioned, so no one ever knew where she had been for those three days, or what she had been doing or who she had been with.

This behaviour inflicted fear and absolute terror in my husband, a deep-rooted fear and anxiety that he still suffers to control today, she had total disregard for how her behaviour affected the people around her including her own mother and young son.

This was not a one-off instance either, she did things like this all the time, she regularly just took off with no mention of where she was going or who she was with, my fiancé would come home from work to find her not in the flat most days, she was living the life of a single person just coming and going as she pleased and not answering to anyone, she was behaving like she didn't have any ties to anyone and no responsibilities.

By the time my husband left the relationship he was already suffering many emotional, psychological and physical issues, it only became apparent following his departure and with numerous doctor and mental health nurse visits that living with a partner who suffers with narcissistic personality disorder and borderline personality disorders causes mental health issues to the suffering partner was ever mentioned to him, he was recommended for counselling and therapy and with the help of his counsellor it was discovered that he was suffering from the effects of narcissistic abuse. He had never even heard this terminology before hearing it from his doctor, he was diagnosed with general anxiety disorder, complex post traumatic stress disorder (C-PTSD) and depression.

As you can see, my stalker was known to me, even though I had never met her and she had never met me, I knew who she was, but even knowing her identity still didn't stop the fear of having a stalker, I picked up on how terrified my husband was of her, a certain amount of his fear was injected into me also. I had witnessed all her rage calls and all her vile messages to him the whole time we had been together, I had seen the physical and emotional effects she was having on him, I felt helpless, there was nothing I could do to make it all stop for him, all I could do was be there for him to talk it through and comfort him during his low times.

Due to her unreasonable nature, I knew there was no advice I could give him to put an end to his personal suffering, and in all honesty, I don't think I was experienced enough to offer him the support that he needed following such a prolonged vindictive attack on him.

CHAPTER TWO

Effects of Narcissistic Abuse
on our Relationship

Narcissistic abuse is a type of abuse where the person doing all the abusing only cares about themselves, they emotionally dominate and control their victims, they use manipulation and coercion to influence their victims' behaviour to suite themselves. The effects of narcissistic abuse can affect the victims in different ways, depending on how long they have had to endure the relationship will determine whether the effects on them are mild and can be overcome, or whether the effects are more severe, and the victim is left with lifelong damage.

Anxiety

Many survivors of narcissistic abuse suffer with anxiety, my husband experienced extreme fear and anxiety in our relationship, and the first year was very challenging for us, it meant we couldn't just make plans and go out with friends for a meal or meet up in a pub for a few after work drinks, he was terrified of absolutely every social event we attended for a while. He suffered regular panic attacks and anxiety attacks, one attack led to him suffering a massive asthma attack that led to him having to be resuscitated on the way to hospital in the back of the ambulance, narcissistic abuse is a serious concern for anyone who has suffered from it.

Depression

My husband was diagnosed with depression after it became apparent that he was struggling with feelings of worthlessness following his exe constantly telling him how useless he was, her constant barrage of messages all contained horrific abuse belittling him and calling him stupid, she ridiculed him and made fun of him, she gaslighted him into reacting, poking him to make him lose his temper with the things she was saying, but he never did lose his temper with her, and never, not once did he ever retaliate against her either, he resilience really amazed me, I was so proud of him for remaining calm during their interactions.

Post-Traumatic Stress Disorder And Complex-Post-Traumatic Stress Disorder

Our doctor diagnosed my husband with complex post-traumatic stress disorder (C-PTSD) his brain was always in fight of flight mode, he was overanxious about everything, he had physical symptoms every time something triggered him regarding his exe. He would break out in a sweat, not be able to breathe properly and told me he felt like he was going to die. Because his exe had put him in a constant state of panic and fear he never knew what she was going to do next, this pushed him into being over vigilant and was in constant fear of her appearing out of nowhere all the time. He found it very hard to relax.

He started to avoid certain people and places that he had enjoyed going out to before, but now he was not able to visit anywhere or talk to anyone, he was paranoid that she was going to get him.

Loss Of Self

My husband had totally lost himself, he had no confidence in himself at all, despite me encouraging him saying he did something well, no matter how much I told him I was proud of him he just never believed me, even the things he had been doing for years competently enough he just couldn't manage anymore. He suffered massive trust issues, not just with his friends but with me also, because he had been constantly gaslighted and lied to, he found it hard to believe me when I told him anything. This really upset me because I felt I was being punished for what his exe had done to him and it was nothing to do with me, I don't behave that way at all.

He started to blame himself for causing it all, and for not standing up to her sooner, it took a lot of convincing from me, his doctor and his counsellor to make him believe that none of it was his fault. He had awful trouble trying to make decisions, he would faff for ages, I got wise to this and pushed him to make decisions more in our relationship as I knew he needed to feel like he had the control back on some things. He was left feeling so low that his exe had convinced him that he couldn't do anything great anymore, we climbed a mountain on our honeymoon, at the bottom looking up he thought he couldn't get to the top, half way up his confidence started getting better, once he was stood at the top of Ben Nevis, he was absolutely elated that he had managed to get to the top!

Cognitive Issues

My husband suffered with a lack of focus and concentration, he was receiving hundreds of abusive messages from his exe daily, she distracted him so much that he couldn't hold focus for very long, his mobile was constantly pinging, in the first few months of their relationship ending he suffered a major car accident, almost cut his finger off using a circular saw and suffered a massive asthma attack. He constantly asked me to keep repeating things I said to him, he couldn't remember anything we had talked about, when I researched this annoying thing that was happening it said victims of narcissistic abuse experience memory loss, especially short-term memory loss, the reason for this was the brain releases surges in stress hormones when you are traumatises, it affects the part of the brain known as the hippocampus region. Continued narcissistic abuse can cause brain damage!

Physical And Emotional Symptoms

As mentioned before my husband suffered anxiety attacks that left him feeling like he was going to die, he would freeze rigid to the spot that he was having the attack in, he would break out in a sweat all over his body and would struggle to breathe, the terror he felt during one of these attacks was huge. His emotions were all over the place, he would be irritable one minute then ok the next, his constant mood swings left me feeling disjointed and unable to keep up with him sometimes.

Trust Issues

My husband's trust was pretty much non-existent to begin with, he still struggles with trust issues today, and I think this will take a long time for him to resolve, if he ever does at all, after being lied to and never knowing what was going to happen on a day-to-day basis, he lost all faith in everyone around him, he thought everyone was lying to him and that he couldn't believe or trust anyone at all. He also had this constant fear of being abandoned due to past experiences with his exe.

He would question everything I said, repeatedly, I felt like he was trying to catch me out lying when I was telling the truth, it caused many rows in the beginning of our relationship.

Fear of What Other People Thought of Him

My husband became so fixated with what other people thought of him, his exe had begun a smear campaign on him, she was talking to anyone who would listen to her, she bad mouthed him to everyone, and he became so paranoid that everyone he knew would hate him because of it. It took a lot of convincing him that the people who knew him and loved him would never be influenced by gossip and scare mongering.

I could see the effects of his previous relationship and I was totally at a loss on how to help him manage his trauma that he had suffered, all the normal family things we were doing together were just not working on resolving his deep rooted issued that he had been left with.

We would go out somewhere nice for the day, he would smile and laugh and be happy at the time but once we arrived back home again, he would slip back into this different version of himself. Recognising the effects is not enough to fix the effects and we both just thought that the longer he was away from her the better he would get, but he didn't.

I began researching online looking up symptoms and effects of an abusive exe partner and how to overcome the trauma, but nothing we applied seemed to be working. My husband attended counselling and we bought lots of self-help books.

The main reason why nothing was working was his exe refused to leave him in peace, she continued with messaging him every day with her vile abusive messages. He maintained contact with her because she was carrying a child that she claimed was his, on the day he left she had claimed she was pregnant with his baby. At first, he thought this was another one of her tactics to make him go back to her, but she sent proof of doing a pregnancy test and it showed as positive.

She wouldn't accept that their relationship was over and that he didn't want to go back to her, he tried to assure her that he would stand by her if the child was his and that he would take ownership of her upbringing, she weaponised the baby from day one, threatening that if he didn't go back to her he would never see the baby, she used every trick she could to try to get him to go back to her, but he stood his ground and told her the relationship was over and for the following 10 months she made his life a living hell, her reasoning behind her abuse towards him was that he left her and the baby was hers and not his, she told him that she was the one creating life and it had nothing to do with him, she let him attend one scan then banned him from all further scans, every time he tried to ask after the welfare of the baby all he got was more abuse, the whole conversations were entirely focused on his exe, she gave no thought towards him or the baby at all, she threatened to kill herself and the baby unless he went back to her.

Now people may say here that she was totally within her rights to be angry that my husband left her, she even told people he left her knowing she was pregnant to show him in a bad light, but he didn't know anything about her being pregnant until after he had left, and her unreasonable behaviour had been happening for years "before" she became pregnant too! He had messages on his phone going back to two years before he left, all vile and vindictive with the sole intention of playing mental mind games with him.

After he had left the relationship there were rumours circulating regarding the parentage of the baby, he was being told that his exe girlfriend had been secretly dating his best friend, this kind of thing happens all the time with people, and more so when a relationship is in trouble and both parties are not happy. He had a gut feeling that she was already seeing someone else way before he left too.

It was clear that she needed urgent medical help for her mental condition, she had been medically diagnosed with borderline personality disorder and mood disorder, but she always refused to accept that anything was wrong with her, she would never seek help, even when other people pointed out that she needed it.

When doing our research we read many articles written by medically trained professionals that clearly stated people with borderline personality disorder and narcissistic personality disorder rarely seek professional help for their condition, mainly because they cannot admit they have an issue at all, they deflect blame onto others and say the problem never lies with them it always lies with other people around them making them behave in inappropriate ways, counsellors are reluctant to take on a person diagnosed with NPD as the counsellors are not able to reason with them and get them to accept that the counsellors professional diagnosis is correct.

In the rare occasions where a person suffering with NPD does approach professionals it is usually for a symptom of narcissistic personality disorder like depression and not the actual disorder itself, they refuse to accept that they are at fault and need help, it becomes useless trying to offer any kind of help and assistance, so they only ever get treated for a symptom of the condition and never the root cause of their issues.

He kept trying to reason with her, right up until he received a load of upsetting abuse one afternoon, his exe sent him a photo of her in the back of an ambulance accusing him of stressing the baby and if anything happened to the baby, she threatened him saying she would find him and kill him, she had constantly been threatening to kill herself and the baby throughout her pregnancy, and this was the point at which he totally broke, he could no longer endure the abuse she was throwing at him any longer, he sent her a message asking her not to contact him and he blocked her.

He sat on the settee with his head in his hands, he was shaking from head to foot, he looked at me and told me he couldn't take the abuse anymore. He was living in constant fear of her killing herself, he told me he had to block her, he had spent months trying to talk to her and trying to get her to see reason, but he just couldn't, and now he felt so bad for the little baby he was terrified the baby may not survive, he was also terrified that his exe was going to come looking for him and kill him like she had said she was going to whether the baby survived or not, he was sitting there in absolute fear of his life. I attempted to calm him down and told him he had done the right thing by blocking her, and maybe give her some time to have the baby and settle down a bit, wait for her emotions to level back out again and then unblock her and see is he can reason with her after that.

He did unblock her five days later after his sister rang him to say she had received a message from his exe saying she had given birth to the baby, she had lied to his sister trying to make him look bad yet again, she had messaged his sister saying that she had informed him she was in premature labour with the baby and all he did was block her, which was a total lie, she never mentioned to his sister that she had sent her usual abusive messages to him and he had totally broken down that day, the messages she did send that day never mentioned anything about being in premature labour they were just abusive vile threats to hurt and maim him.

He was always painted in a bad light to everyone she spoke to, twisting every single situation against him, she was always setting him up to look like the bad guy, all she did say that day was that the baby was showing signs of being distressed and she was being taken to hospital, followed by a nasty threat.

The whole time during their time together he had found that he had to constantly defend himself to people that his exe was always lying to, and even after the end of their relationship it was still exactly the same hateful lies she was spreading to his family and friends about him, and in this instance it was no different to the many times before in the past, he found himself trying to defend himself and clear his name yet again.

Once he had unblocked her to ask after her and the baby, boy did he wish he hadn't, she instantly launched into yet another verbal attack on him, she immediately called him and proceeded to scream at him down the phone calling him stupid and insensitive to her needs, she told him she had suffered a condition called Meconium Aspiration Syndrome (MAS) and it was all his fault he caused it, she started screaming the "C Bomb" word at him, it was her favourite word, she used it all the time, she began calling him all the names under the sun, he couldn't even get a word in edgeways, he was trying so hard to calm her down and talk to her but he couldn't, so he ended the call, the moment he ended the call with her she started sending another load of abusive messages, it led to him blocking her yet again.

When we looked up the condition known as Meconium Aspiration Syndrome (MAS) we discovered it is where a baby poops in the womb and the faeces gets taken into the lungs of the unborn child via the amniotic fluid and can cause damage to the lungs.

If this happens during pregnancy there is no other option but to urgently deliver the baby, it is a traumatic and extremely stressful situation, again we understood that, but this condition was NOT caused by the father, it has NEVER in medical history ever been caused by any of the fathers of any of the babies born in this manner.

In fact this medical condition is caused by several factors and they are ALL related to the health of the mother and NOT the father, on examination of the mother all of the following applied, the mother was an older mother aged 38 at the time of getting herself pregnant, she was morbidly obese weighing in at 119kg and only being 5ft 2in means she is considered to be extremely overweight, she didn't follow a good diet as she regularly ate take aways and wasn't eating healthily at all consuming foods high in saturated fats with extremely high sugar contents, she didn't do any form of regular exercise at all, she led a very sedentary lifestyle, she was suffering with blood pressure issues due to her large frame and she also had gestational diabetes along with gestational primary biliary cholangitis, and one other factor that can contribute to Meconium Aspiration Syndrome is an infection in the mother carrying the child, again nothing to do with the father at all, but this didn't stop her from sending vile abusive messages saying that the baby was stressed, when my husband tried to stand up for himself and attempted to reason with her, every time he tried to explain there was a difference between the baby being "stressed" and in "distress" she just threw back a load of unreasonable abuse and was not just a little upset but violently angry and aggressive towards him with narcissistic rage.

The reason for her having to have the baby delivered earlier than planned was all due to her actions and not the father at all, it was yet another example of her deflecting all her rage onto him yet again, he broke down and just couldn't handle being treated this way, so he blocked her again, he was just receiving threat after threat and he was living his life in constant fear of her ludicrous accusations and empty threats.

He was advised by his counsellor to break contact with her entirely and to not make direct contact with her at all, but after a few weeks of her not being able to abuse him, she messaged his sister again begging for her to get him to unblock her so she could talk to him, his sister passed on her message so he unblocked her again, thinking that she had calmed down enough to be able to talk to her sensibly.

What can I say! "hoovering" at its absolute best here, using a baby as a weapon to terrorise and control him through fear.

She begged him to go and see the baby at the hospital, she berated him saying all the other dads are there except for him, she failed to realise that he wasn't there as a direct result of her lies, accusations and continued abuse, again he was blamed for not being there, she used emotional blackmail to guilt trip him into being controlled by her yet again, her messages were relentless, she kept harassing him until he gave in, so he agreed to go see the baby, once he got there, you guessed it, she launched into yet another verbal attack on him accusing him of not caring and being an arsehole, he took her a gift, a tiny baby grow and bib for the baby with a cute soft toy and two boxes of chocolates for her, but she just tossed it to one side, and later she dropped it all on his mums doorstep, minus the boxes of chocolates, saying she didn't want it and that she will buy the baby everything she needs and he can f@@@ off, then accused him of not buying the baby anything.

He couldn't win no matter what he did, if he went to see the baby, he was wrong, and if he didn't go to see the baby, he was wrong, if he bought her something he was wrong, if he didn't buy her anything he was wrong, he was being yo-yod constantly and it was breaking him.

He relayed all of this behaviour to this counsellor who advised him to break contact, his mental health was seriously at risk at this point, so on the advice of his counsellor he blocked her yet again.

It was obvious now that the relationship had totally broken down and it was best for all concerned to break the contact totally there was no reasoning with her, she had shown how unreasonable she was, and he had seen this for years in their relationship, she just made bad situations even worse.

He had been asking to see the baby for a month after she was born but was refused access, he had constantly asked to see the baby and was constantly refused access, his exe had become more abusive towards him following the birth of the child, and he had been left with no choice but to involve external help, so he made an application to the National Association of Child Contact Centres (NACCC) so he could see the baby without the mother being present, the NACCC offer a service to parents who are not able to effectively communicate with each other to be able to make amicable access arrangements to see the children they share together through the staff at the centres, the way it works is, the baby would be dropped to the centre by the mother then she would leave, the father would arrive and get to see the baby in the presence of the centre staff, then he would leave and the mother would return to collect the baby.

All contact and arrangements between the two parents are handled by the centre staff, ensuring that the parents never need to make direct contact with each other, it ensures the safety, and the needs of the children are first and foremost, it elevates the priority of the children's needs above all others. These centres recognise that children have needs too and if they are not being met due to one parent being awkward and withholding access from the other parent then this is a great way of maintaining contact with children.

Once my husband had paid to register with this service, he was given a reference number and a link to send to his exe via email, it clearly stated within his email that all she had to do was click the link and register with the NACCC and all communication could stop between them and the centre would take over all communications between both parties so they don't need to speak to each other at all, but she replied back to his email refusing to register and to take her to court. She told him his name wasn't on the birth certificate and he had no rights what so ever, her reply was vile and nasty, she never had any intensions of ever letting him see the baby, she was only using the child as a weapon against him, exactly the same as she had done previously with her first child too, she had not allowed his father access to him for the first 8 years of his life, she had ensured in that time that she had sufficiently poisoned her son enough against his father too with no hopes of ever establishing a healthy relationship between the two of them, and she was doing exactly the same again with her second child's father too.

It was now that she discovered he was engaged to me! And my husband's abuser became my stalker!

Once she knew my identity she proceeded to stalk my social

media, she removed pictures of myself and my family and emailed them to my husband abusing him, calling both him and me the vilest of names, now we had been sensitive to her predicament, we had been discrete about our relationship together, and here she was absolutely raging about him daring to not only leave her the previous year, but to start a new relationship with someone else.

*How dare he leave an abusive toxic relationship
and start a healthy one with someone else?*

She accused him of seeing me before their relationship had ended which was a lie she told herself and others, it made her feel better having someone else to blame for her bad behaviour, and by blaming someone else for the demise in her relationship it meant that she was absolved of any blame towards their breakup whatsoever! It meant she could play the victim to others, and now with the lies she was telling herself and others she felt it gave her a valid reason to continue to abuse and harass her exe partner and now target his new partner too.

She refused to accept she played any part in the ending of their relationship saying that they were working on fixing things before he left, hence how she came to be pregnant, she was not being totally honest with herself which made trying to reason with her even harder, in her head she was believing her fabricated lies, and she was creating this whole false scenario where she was the constant victim, she attempted to involve others in her drama saga, she immediately started a smear campaign on me and my family and set to work trying to destroy my good name.

My husband was fearfully embarrassed by her behaviour, and he promised he would get her to stop and leave me alone, so he tried to reason with her yet again, upon discovering he was seeing someone else, he went from receiving hundreds of messages a day to receiving "hundreds" of messages in the space of a few hours, he told me he was just going to let her rant and get it all out of her system, he assured me that she would calm down, and I don't know what made me believe what he was saying, especially after I had witnessed her abusing him for months beforehand! He had showed me messages that went back two years before their relationship had ended and I had seen all the messages she had sent him after their relationship ended too!

But somehow, I held onto the hope of him being able to reason with her and get her to stop.

After three more weeks of constant abuse and thousands of vile messages with her abusing him, me and my family, he blocked her for good and told her not to message him anymore.

We mistakenly thought that would be the end of it, but it wasn't, once my husband had blocked her number she used her sons mobile to message him, so he blocked that number too, and again we thought that would be the end of it all but it wasn't, she got one of her friends to message him, her friend left vile voice messages on his mobile, and on his sisters mobile too, it was at this point that I messaged both my husband's exe and her newly involved friend I politely asked them both to mind their own business and to stop stalking my social media and leave me and my family alone, I wasn't surprised when I received abusive voice clips from her friend, so I blocked his exe, her son and her friends mobile numbers, I didn't want to receive further abuse from any of them.

Again, I mistakenly thought that would be the end of it all and that I wouldn't hear from any of them ever again, but how wrong could I have been, no one could have seen what was going to happen next.

It was now October that year and we had been receiving abuse for a period of 10 months solid, it was time to put a stop to it all, I told my husband I was going to the police, he wasn't getting her to listen to him and she wasn't stopping her behaviour at all, his counsellor had also advised approaching the police, so I did.

When the police visited our house, they listened to what we told them, they said they see this all the time, they advised us to send a "Cease and Desist" email to my husband's exe, the email firmly stated that any contact from her or her friends would be seen as unwanted contact and would be seen as harassment and reported to the police, we sent this email to his exe while the police were sat with us, surprisingly my husband's exe replied back, the police read the reply and advised us not to reply, and any further messages we received would be seen as harassment and she could be arrested.

I think at this point my husband just felt relieved that someone else was going to step in and offer help and support in handling the whole sorry situation with her, I could see the relief in him, his abuser had become so used to abusing him that she never thought he would report her to the authorities, she thought she could just get away with treating him appallingly and he would just stay silent and never reach out for help.

Again it didn't stop there, he received a further email from his exe accusing me of sending her a nasty text message calling her fat, she had taken a screen shot of it on her phone and emailed it to him, he didn't reply back, he followed the advice of the police, and about an hour later he received another email from her accusing me of sending a second text message calling her fat again, she had taken another screen shot of the message on her phone threatening to go to the police, so we reported this to the police to save her the trouble.

The police held the opinion that it was attention seeking behaviour whereby his exe was attempting to stay connected to him and remain in contact, it was a tactic used by many people harassing victims trying to discredit their names and make them look bad to others, the police arrested her under caution, they took her to the police station and questioned her about what was happening, she denied abusing us, but when the police produced evidence of us being abused and it was coming from her email address after we had specifically asked her to stop messaging, she then admitted she had done this and agreed to leave us alone.

Excellent we thought, now after a year of receiving abuse from her, she will stop!

CHAPTER THREE

Things Got Worse

After reporting everything to the police we thought that would be the end of it, we enjoyed a week of peace and quiet, even though we did jump when our phones went off, but we eventually began to relax a bit more.

Then the withheld number silent phone calls started happening, it started off with a few a day, then a few in the middle of the night, then it became a daily happening, every time we answered the phone we were met with total silence, but we could hear someone at the other end of the phone, so we started not answering the calls.

We started to receive WhatsApp messages from unrecognised numbers, asking us silly questions on what we were wearing, and do we want to hook up tonight, so we started blocking those numbers too. We reported everything to the police and were advised to record it all, so we began taking screen shots and printing it all off and filing it in folders.

We started to receive an unusually large amount of Facebook friend requests and Instagram requests. When we looked at the profiles, some were freshly created accounts only minutes old with no information and no details or friends on them, so we started rejecting the friend requests, within minutes the same profiles had sent new friend requests, so we again deleted them, once we received a third request we blocked them, only to have another one take its place in a totally new name and again minutes old, so we started to report the accounts for bullying and harassment, then we blocked them.

This continued of for about another week, I started to receive direct messages asking me about my life and where I worked, I knew it was my husband's exe and her friend who had phoned me and left vile voice messages on my phone, so I reported the messages as harassment and blocked them.

I set up call blocking on my phone, but I had to answer the private number calls as they were either the police or my doctor's surgery, occasionally they caught me out, but not very often, and if they did, I would just hang up, it was more of a nuisance at this point than a direct threat.

I just thought that eventually they would just get bored and leave me alone, but I was wrong, they didn't leave me alone at all, they did the opposite, they got a lot worse.

Over time they were discovering more information about me, they used any information they were able to find on me to target me further. They looked up all my social media accounts and proceeded to stalk me online. I started to receive fake friend requests with newly created accounts on my Instagram now too as well as my Facebook account, the I started receiving quick adds on my Snapchat account too. It was obvious to me and the police that this was both my husbands exe and her friend.

We kept taking screen shots and reporting to the police.

We came out to go to work one morning only to discover my husbands' tires had been let down on his van, and it wasn't long before this became a regular occurrence involving all our vehicles. We started carrying an electric pump in the boot so we could pump them back up and still get to work on time.

All coincidental, until you see her driving past your house smirking at you! She wanted us to know it was her doing it, it was her attempt to intimidate us both.

We just thought she would get fed up and eventually stop.

Once she knew what vehicle mine was, my tires started to get let down too! What a surprise, I was beginning to get annoyed with her now, why is a grown woman terrorising another woman like this, what is she trying to achieve? If she had a problem with me, why didn't she just come and talk to me face to face? What is the point of all this childishness?

The silent phone calls increased, they were annoying by this point, and we had just moved into the month of September, my birthday month.

My husband's exe had pretty much become my stalker by this point, and I was seeing her everywhere I was going too, the withheld numbers were constant and the fake friend requests had become the daily norm for me now too! It was clear I was intentionally being stalked, harassed and antagonised and I knew the worst thing I could do was retaliate in any way.

One morning I came out to go to work and one of my tires had been let down as usual, but I also noticed a puddle of some kind of fluid underneath my front wheel, didn't think much of it, got in the car and proceeded to head towards work, got to work ok, and at the end of the day was on my way home travelling along the motorway when I noticed my car had a bit of a floaty feeling to it, I applied the brakes to find there was nothing there and my car wasn't stopping, the next thing I knew was my front calliper ceased on and my front wheel locked, as I was travelling on one of the new smart motorways there wasn't a recovery lane for me to pull into so I had to drive my car at 10mph for 2 miles to get to the exit to enable me to get off the motorway, cars were zooming past me so fast, a few almost hit me, horns were being blasted at me, but there was nowhere for me to pull in or get out of my car safely, I was left with no other way of getting my car off the motorway other than slowly driving it off in total fear of being hit from behind by a vehicle travelling at 70mph.

Once I was safely off the motorway and a recovery lane was visible, I immediately pulled over and got out to take a look, the front disc was glowing red it smelt of burning and I knew it was at risk of setting on fire, I had to wait an hour for it to cool down before I started trying to drive it for the remaining few miles home, which I drove in short stages with my hazard lights on. After getting the car home, my son called his friend who is a mechanic and he came to look at it, and after close inspection he informed us that the car would need a whole new front end as the damage was quite extensive, he said I was lucky to have escaped alive as the damage caused to my car could have led to a catastrophic outcome, it could have led to my death and to the deaths of many other road users that day. I have always owned high powered sports cars, and I have always had all my vehicles regularly serviced as and when they needed to be, and my mechanic had only performed a full service including changing the brake pads three weeks prior to this happening, he confirmed that all the brake linings and connections were all perfectly ok at the time of servicing and nothing needed renewing or changing. With this in mind, we immediately reported this to the police.

We were advised to apply for a Non-Molestation Order with a Restraining Order that carried the Powers of Arrest, and informed that if anything further happened we could have our stalker arrested and charged, so we applied for the order and a date was given of December 1st that same year.

My husband attended court, his exe denied everything, as expected, my husband also raised the issue he had experienced attempting to see his child, so the Judge ordered that there was to be no direct or indirect contact between them both, and no one was to encourage any third party to make direct or indirect contact and if this was to happen it would be seen as a breach of the court conditions being agreed to on this date.

The Judge also ordered access arrangements for visitation rights to be arranged via an agreed third party, who was a friend of my husbands exe to ensure he had regular access to the baby his exe claimed was his. The Judge ordered that a DNA test was to be carried out to ascertain whether he was the father or not.

This order was granted on the 1st December 2022 and was in place until the following December 2023, it came as no surprise to us that our stalker did not adhere to any of the promises she made to the Judge that day in court and she proceeded to break all the contents of the order, no arrests on her were ever made by the police, no charges for failure to comply were ever made and no convictions were made as a result of her breaches either, we felt the order was a total waste of our time and money.

Within two days of the hearing my husband received a Child Support Agency (CSA) letter saying his exe had applied for child support and named him as the father of her child. The CSA staff advised him that if he had any doubts about being the father of the child that he could order a DNA test to be carried out, he was informed by the CSA that he would have to pay the costs of obtaining a DNA test, and if it was found that he was not the father that the cost would be transferred to the mother. So, he agreed to pay the costs and he asked the CSA to plan for the test to be carried out.

Two days later, we received a letter from the CSA informing us that his exe had withdrawn her claim!

> *Hang on a minute, what women withdraws*
> *a CSA claim and refuses a DNA test?*

The CSA informed my husband that he was no longer liable to pay for the child as the parentage had not been proven and he was released from the claim that had been made against him.

Receiving this news from the CSA that the claim had been removed by her just seemed to confirm the rumours regarding the child not being his and may be the child of the man people were reporting she was having a secret affair with, we felt she had rolled that lie as far as she could without the truth being uncovered.

All our family and friends were telling us that our answer regarding the parentage of the child could be found in the withdrawal of the claim, we were being told that we had had a lucky escape and to be grateful that would be the end of it all now and we could just go on with our lives with peace of mind.

But we didn't receive peace of mind, we just went back to not knowing whether the child was indeed my husbands, or another mans, we didn't get the answers we so desperately needed, and his exe knew that too, it was yet another one of her cruel mind games, specifically designed to mess with his mental health.

He was now destined to spend years waiting for his answers, to be in constant emotional turmoil, forever wondering if the baby was his or not, how can a woman be so cruel to another human being? All the years he could have played a big part in her life but was intentionally excluded specifically for the cruel pleasure of the mother, exactly as she had done with her first child too.

She knew by not naming him on the birth certificate that he would have no say in her life at all, and she knew he would have no control on whether he got to see her or not too, and she intentionally used this fact to play head games with him.

How many mothers have done this to absent father on purpose, men who were already being great dads to their children up until the breakdown of their relationship with the mothers, and those who have been robbed of the chance to ever establish a healthy relationship with their children? Why is nothing being done about this? Why aren't we talking more about this, and raising awareness?

Needless to say, we continued to receive harassment all over the Christmas period, the daily withheld number calls and the social media fake friend requests also continued, the direct messages on my social media continued along with the tires being let down on our vehicles, we had our Christmas decorations that we had put outside our house vandalised too, so we installed CCTV and a home alarm system, this stopped all the tires on the vehicles being let down, and it stopped any damaged being done to our house too.

Again, thinking that would be the end of their campaign.

January saw the beginning of a new harassment tactic, it was the beginning of the snapchat snaps, false accounts made and within minutes of being made we started receiving quick adds, they were taking screen shots of our snap profiles sending one direct message calling us names then changing the name on the account so we couldn't reply back or search the profile to report it, we received hundreds of these in the month of January......... hundreds! Who has the time to harass on this level?

After reporting it all to the police my stalker was arrested under caution for the second time, she was questioned about what was happening, again she denied it was her doing it, she was released on bail until the following April, and upon her release she immediately deactivated all her social media accounts in her name, she also disconnected her mobile number too.

This was a futile attempt by her to hide the accounts she had been caught using to harass my husband and me with, she had been caught out, we had proved that she was directly linked to what was happening to us, and we could prove without a doubt that it was her and her friend, the police knew all their social media account names and their mobile numbers, and even though we had them all blocked on everything they still managed to make direct and indirect contact with us.

We noticed a direct shift in the harassment following my stalkers second arrest, all the harassment that my husband had been receiving from her and her friend stopped, just stopped! But it increased for me and continued relentlessly for the next few years.

Oh, lucky me!

February was exceptionally bad with Valentines Day being the worst day of the whole month, I received hateful cards personally addressed to me through the post, delivered direct to my door. The online harassment continued in the form of the withheld numbers, more fake friend requests and instant adds on snapchat. My abuse and harassment folder had grown from one A4 ring binder folder into two.

I knew I was being specifically targeted and there wasn't anything I could do about it, my mobile was constantly pinging with messages and alerts, my social media was being hit by fake accounts and fake requests. As fast as I was reporting them more were appearing, this was getting beyond a joke. I had removed all personal photos off my background and profile pictures on all my social media accounts, I had replaced them with ordinary everyday objects, like a flower or a flag. I was trying to make my profiles as boring as I possibly could to my stalkers.

But despite all my best efforts the stalking and harassment

continued. I was receiving so much harassment that I had changed reporting everything daily to the police to once per month, I would type up the harassment I received and copy and paste it into the incident online, every month I was given a reference number and that is as far as it all went.

I continued to report the harassment monthly via the police online reporting system, I would print off the reply email that said thank you for reporting your crime, I would be given a new crime reference number and just filed that in my folders where I was printing everything off, so it was all being kept together.

We all concluded that because my stalker was not happy in her life, she was going out of her way to try bringing me down to her miserable level, she didn't want me being happy at all, and her stalking and harassment campaign was meant to make damn sure that I wasn't happy either.

The harder she worked at trying to hurt me and destroy my happiness the harder I had to work to maintain it. My stalker assumed (**it's dangerous to assume things as the word assume equates to Assuming Makes An ASS of U and ME**) that she could terrorise me just like she had done to my husband for many years.

The beginning of March saw even more abuse, the silent phone calls had increased in volume, I was now receiving on average 20 calls a day, my stalker had added my mobile number to cold callers lists and I started to receive lots of spam phone calls too, these were mainly for double glazing or courses that she had made enquiries on and filled in my details to make contact with me, I put my spam blocker on to reduce the amount of calls I was getting, the social media fake profiles and fake friend requests escalated, and my stalker and her friend were both attempting to get added onto my accounts, all my social media accounts were locked down to friends only and marked as private, no one unless they are on my friends list are able to see any of my private posts and was driving her wild with an unhealthy curiosity, she was driven by a need to know what I was doing, where I was going, what hobbies I had and not knowing any of this information was just fuelling her obsession with me even more, the less she knew the more she wanted to know.

I knew it was her and her friend doing all of this, but since my stalkers second arrest at the beginning of the year, after deactivating her social media accounts and her mobile so nothing could be directly traced back to her, she had started using throw away mobiles and sim cards, the numbers that were being used to harass me the police investigated and informed me were all unregistered newly activated numbers, coincidently all on the same mobile network that my stalker and her friend were registered to! How strange is that! (this is known as English sarcasm, not everyone gets it)

We were informed by the police that it would be extremely hard to prove any of the harassment we were receiving via these numbers could be directly linked to my stalker and her friend and that the police didn't have the resources to track and trace all the calls we were receiving, so we reached yet another dead end, we were disappointed that there would not be a firm prosecution with it all.

Even blocking her, her family and her friends who were known to us on every social media platform and every mobile number she rang me from or messaged me with didn't stop her, she just found different ways to menace me, she went to great lengths to find out who my friends were and she started targeting them too, she was messaging my friends asking personal questions about me and my family, and she continued attempting to get added to my friends social media accounts too, she still uses this method to attempt to connect with me, she thinks that by just one of my friends adding her onto their social media will enable her to see my posts, but she still won't be able to see anything I post as my privacy settings are set to "friends only"

It didn't stop her trying though, she kept trying to get information on me so she could continue to stalk me after I kept blocking her, she was relentless, she just kept creating numerous fake accounts with fake names and proceeded to stalk and harass me and my friends using this method.

No matter how many times we reported the numbers and the

names of the accounts or the tags they were using, the same answers were being given to us by the police, they didn't have the resources to handle a harassment case of this size.

It became obvious that my stalker was becoming obsessed with me and my life, she was going to any lengths to connect with me the fact that my stalker and her friend were so obsessed with trying to annoy me, I knew they were attempting to gaslight me into reacting, and I also knew that the moment I reacted or retaliated against them I would be seen as the one in the wrong, and that if I did crack and react the way they wanted me to that it would reinforce their lies to others and make people think that they were the true victims like they were making themselves out to be, so no matter how hard they worked at trying to provoke me I knew I had to maintain control on my emotions at all times.

They were both working so hard at trying to get me to retaliate too, it became so funny in the end, once I had worked out what they were doing, how they were doing it and why they were doing it, it just took away all their power over me.

The psychology behind why people antagonize their targets is far reaching, and I only began to brush the surface of why they were doing what they were doing to me, I was looking at the whole situation with a normal rational head on my shoulders, and I thought that I was dealing with people that would eventually see the error of their ways, that with time they would come to their senses and stop behaving so badly.

In the beginning I made excuses for her stalking and harassing behaviour, I kept telling myself that she was in shock, that she was attempting to process an awful lot of information following the ending of her relationship with my husband, she was experiencing a lot of life changes being pregnant at a time that should have been one of the happiest moments of her life but now instead of being in a committed relationship she had found herself alone and facing the daunting task of raising a child on her own as a single parent, I told myself she must be struggling to process what had happened, I sympathised with her, I tried to imagine what it must be like for her being an older woman who was struggling with her mental health and not being in the best of health physically either must be presenting her will all kinds of daily challenges.

I found I was beginning to excuse her behaviour and I was setting myself up for further harassment and abuse, I was turning into one of her enablers, I was allowing her to get away with treating me badly, I don't struggle setting firm boundaries with people and I most certainly don't accept bad behaviour towards me from family and friends, so I why should I accept it from her? The truth is, I shouldn't accept this kind of behaviour from her or anyone else EVER!

The problem wasn't with my ability to set firm boundaries, instead the problem was trying to reason with unreasonable abusive toxic people, that is where the issue came from. I knew in my mind right from the start that trying to deal with this situation was going to prove to be extremely difficult.

My husband constantly blamed himself for what was happening and they way she was, I had to reinforce that fact that he was not to blame for how she behaved nor was he to blame for anything she said either, she was a grown woman and she had to take responsibility for her own words and actions, he had no control over her, he only had control over himself, and he should not be apologising on her behalf.

The truth of the matter was, my stalker and her friend held very high opinions of themselves, they never admitted when they were wrong, they believed they were better than everyone else, and deflected all blame onto anyone else they could target, including me. Neither of them had a large circle of friends, and they never questioned why people didn't like them at all, they could never accept they had done anything wrong or caused any stress in any of their interactions with people, and instead of looking at themselves a bit closer and accepting any blame for their behaviour all they did was blame others for the way they were instead.

I worked out their characters very quickly once their smear campaign was launched on me, and their grandiose attitudes they held regarding themselves was the main reason why I could never get them to see things from a different point of view, they never saw themselves as the issue, or the cause of the problem, they deflected that entirely onto me, I knew they would never admit they had done anything wrong and I also knew that I would never receive an apology out of either of them either. They had convinced themselves they were in the right and that I deserved to be stalked and harassed by them too.

I also came to realise that they were both fuelling each other's bad behaviour and that they were both as bad as each other, trying to reason with one person who is unreasonable is bad enough, let alone two people who share the same mindset, that was proving to be darn near impossible.

I had hoped that maybe the friend of my stalker could be reasoned with, that as her friend she would want my stalker to move on with her life and accept that things are they way they are through no fault of anyone else, but I soon realised that my stalkers friend had been brainwashed into acting as her mutt and coerced into attacking me in tandem with my stalker.

I had no idea on what I could do to get these two women to stop stalking and harassing me, everything I could think of I had already tried.

CHAPTER FOUR

All Mouth and No Trousers

Not once did my stalker come face to face with me, she used the threats and verbal abuse as a screen to hide herself behind, spewing out her rage and animosity towards me, attempting to terrorise me into allowing her to hold power and control over me, and the less I reacted to her empty threats the worse her behaviour got.

I was amazed at the lengths she was going to trying to obtain information on me and my family, she even dropped a tracker on my car, trackers are now so small if they are placed on your vehicles there is no way of seeing them at all, I thought it was strange that every time I left my house my stalker would turn up everywhere I went, it really did confuse me as to how she always seemed to know my exact location at any given moment, although sometimes my location was given away by some of my friends on my Facebook, people who had been convinced into disclosing my personal life to my stalker.

I was in two minds about the people who did this to me, knowing my situation with having a stalker, I thought they either had no idea how much this was starting to impact my life and my mental health and that my stalker had been clever in her way of getting my friends to report my movements back to her, because stalkers are very clever in gaining intel on their victims by any means open to them, if a stalker is not able to gain personal information on their target by simple means of online stalking and visiting profiles reading up on you and watching you from a safe distance, then it forces them to use other methods to gain the knowledge they are after.

Seeing as my social media accounts were all locked down

this prevented my stalker from gaining the information that I didn't want her to have on me, but by me locking down my personal information it just forced her to adopt a different approach, so she would message my friends or attempt to get added onto their social media since all her attempts to get on mine had failed, she would sweetly ask after my husband to see what he was doing now and where he was going, and when that didn't work she would approach other friends and even some family members too.

The second view I held was that the people who were directly feeding my stalker personal information on me, I thought must know damn well what they are doing, and that they must have thought it was highly hilarious to divulge my whereabouts to her. These people are what are technically referred to as "flying monkeys" named after the flying monkeys in the film The Wizard Of Oz, the monkeys that were used by the wicked witch to report everything they saw and heard straight back to her, well this is now widely used as the term to describe a person who reports information back to a person they know to be of a nasty nature, they are also referred to as "enablers" they are siding with the stalker, and they are enabling the stalkers behaviour.

I was very disappointed with the people who I had considered to be my friends, people I mistakenly thought I could trust to keep me safe were intentionally giving away personal information about me directly to my stalker, I reached a point where I didn't know who I could trust.

I knew that if I allowed this to continue then I was in for even more stalking and harassment, and by this point I thought my personal safety was being out at high risk, so I closed ranks on everyone very quickly, you find other people love the drama, because if it isn't happening to them, they don't see the seriousness of the situation at all, nor do they understand the impact it has on you and your family nor do they understand how it makes you feel, and I actually thought at this point, they don't care about me either so why should I care too much for them?

I consider myself to be quite a resilient person, but after a long time of being stalked nonstop it can be enough to bring down the toughest of people.

This kind of experience changes you in so many ways, if you have ever been stalked, you just know you are going to change into a different version of yourself, you can never go back to the way you were before your ordeal started either, in the beginning you are able to just flick it off and handle your emotions so much better, like water off a ducks' back, but as time goes on you begin to find yourself changing, you find yourself passing through phases in how you begin dealing with everything, first phase is always denial, you think things that start to happen to you are just a coincidence, but after a while these coincidences start becoming more frequent and you reach a point where you cannot ignore that something strange is happening to you, you can no longer file this under a denial label, and you are forced to admit to yourself that something is not quite right.

You then move to the next phase, this is where your awareness rises and you start to notice things more, its where you become hyper aware and massively over vigilant, you may find yourself becoming a little bit more sensitive to your surroundings, you look around you more, you start to notice the colours of vehicles and the faces of people. You may even start making notes, if you have a mobile phone, you may start taking photos of things you think you are seeing more often, and your brain starts to rocket into overdrive with your heart following suite and beating way faster than it normally does.

Enter the next phase, the paranoid phase, this is the phase where you start to become paranoid about absolutely everything and you start linking everything together in your head, simple things that you never noticed before, you roll back to before any of this started happening to you, things that really have nothing to do with your stalker at all, but you are now making connections in your mind that are not really there, you start to think that everyone around you is out to get you, this is the time you really start to lose your shite! You can no longer hold onto your sense of reality you feel panic rising inside you, you think something awful is going to happen to you, and you begin to question everything until you enter the next phase.

Anger! It's a natural response to what is happening to you and once you enter the anger phase you know things are bad, you start to feel resentment towards the person trying to cause you mental harm, you start to ask yourself "why are they doing this?" "Why me?" "Why don't they just leave me alone?" and you don't have any answers to any of the questions you begin to ask yourself and neither do any of your family and friends, you are totally on your own here and no one is able to help you, you feel isolated and angry at what is happening to you, and you feel this way most of the time too!

You start to explode at the smallest of things, your normal control over your emotions begins slipping, it's at this point that the people closest to you begin to notice changes in your behaviour, they start to see the changes happening to you, changes that were not obvious before, but are starting to play out now, and the funny thing here is, you don't see it at all, you find yourself deflecting the blame onto your stalker at this point, you are angry because of them, they are making you angry and reacting the way you are, technically known as "reactive abuse" your stalker sees this too and it makes them push you even harder, because at this point they now know what they are doing to you is starting to affect you and it makes them feel more superior to you, you have inadvertently handing them the power over you. You become angry at yourself because you feel like you are beginning to lose a grip on yourself, you don't like the changes that are happening to you and you don't like being made to feel the way your stalker is making you feel right now.

Roll on the next phase, the confrontational phase, if your stalker is known to you, as mine was, this is the time where you attempt to reach out to them and ask them directly what they think they are doing, and you will be met with one of two responses from them, the first response is one is denial, your stalker will tell you that you are being weird and crazy and that you are imagining things because they are adamant they are not stalking you at all... and the second response, which is the response I received, is one of total animosity, vileness and abuse, my stalker had convinced herself that her stalking me was totally my fault and she was allowed to stalk me all because I had dared to enter into a relationship with her exe boyfriend after their relationship had ended the year before we got together. How very dare I?

You cannot reason with unreasonable people – fact!

When I began researching why women stalked other women it was mainly out of jealousy and a morbid curiosity of the targeted victim, my research went on to say that many women who stalk other women compare themselves to their target and attempt to mirror their victims holding some kind of twisted view that if they dress like their victim or adopt their lifestyle that they are somehow becoming the person they are stalking.

Women stalk other women for many reasons, one reason is to dominate and control their target through intimidation and fear tactics by terrorising them into being afraid. It gives the stalker a feeling of power and authority, they feel that they are able to control the target and influence them into doing what the stalker wants them to do, they get some kind of sick kick out of watching their target begin changing their behaviour and lifestyle to attempt to avoid the stalkers advances, the stalker revels in the target's misery.

My research also went on to say that women who tend to stalk other women, have a huge sense of failure and inadequacy in their lives, and that their targets have something they are missing in their own lives, and this could be anything from a love interest to a house or vehicle, the stalker sees their target as a person that has achieved all the things they wanted to achieve in life but still have not managed to succeed in obtaining, I knew that my stalker saw her exe partner as her property and that in her mind I didn't deserve to have him.

I understood how her mind was thinking but what I couldn't do was convince her to stop! And I knew that my stalker had recruited others in her hate campaign against me, I knew my stalker and her friend had become obsessed with finding many ways in which they could cause drama and trauma to my life, but again I didn't know how to get them to stop and leave me alone, I thought once the courts and the police had been involved that all the stalking and harassment would just slowly die down and stop completely.

But it wasn't the case, the online stalking became so bad, and I had no way of stopping the methods that were being used to target me, personal photos of me that my stalker and her friend had removed off my social media accounts before I realised what they were doing were being used to sign me up for sex sites, porn sites and dating sites, I only discovered this was happening when a male friend of mine informed me that he had received a message from me on what looked like a personal online dating profile with my name and photos on.

To my horror he was right, my stalker had created numerous dating site profiles using my personal information and I began receiving hook up messages from women as she thought it would be hilarious to sign me up as a lesbian, again my phone was ringing off the hook, my email inbox was stuffed full of dating site emails, sign up emails and personal messages from all the registered users looking to date other females.

She didn't stop here either, she entered my personal details on the dark web and added my name to numerous sex offenders' lists, she registered me for every single dating site known to man, I received hundreds of emails a day all directly hitting my inbox, her and her friend completed online surveys and input my details and ticked the box to opt into receiving offers from other companies so I would receive hundreds of spam emails a day, every single day – for years!

The time it was taking me to block the senders and block all the domains was becoming my normal morning routine, even reporting to my service provider as phishing wasn't working. The admin time taken to keep on top of recording all of this was just ridiculous, but I kept recording it all because the police had told me to do this and that eventually it could all be used as evidence in a harassment case against my stalker and her flying monkeys.

I took screen shots; I made notes on the dates and times it happened and was asked to write a brief description what had happened and how it made me feel. I was determined to see this through to the bitter end and I had my mind set on making damn sure these vindictive women were going to be brought to justice.

Thinking back on how my ordeal escalated so quickly into daily stalking and harassment I came to the conclusion that I didn't think my stalker was able to just cease what she was doing and I began to think that she would never leave me alone.

Her own failures in her life were pushing her to attack me for being successful in life, her delusional state had made her become so obsessed with finding out personal information about me, her need to find out what I looked like, how I dressed, what my frame size what, was I fat or thin, what colour hair did I have, what were my interests and hobbies, where did I go for holidays, her obsessive need to discover every detail about me and my life was pushing her deeper into a sinister obsessive state.

I naively thought that when we applied for the Non-Molestation and Restraining Order that it would put an end to our nightmare, but it didn't at all, it just fuelled her rage even move. All the broken promises you receive from a system that is meant to protect the innocent, a justice system that failed you so terribly that it left you so distraught and not knowing where or who to turn to for support. How do you handle a blow like this?

My stalker and her flying monkeys continued on with no signs of stopping, the abuse that my husband had endured during their relationship together lasted for over four years, then he received a year of abuse from her following the ending of their relationship, then she moved onto stalking and harassing me for a further two years, so we had been recording her abuse for three years!!!

Three draining years! Three years wasted!
Well.................. not exactly.

I got to a point where I stopped recording everything happening to me, I knew what my stalker was doing and I knew exactly how she was doing it, I also knew why she was doing it too, so what did I do about it?

I wrote two books and published them, this book you are reading now, and my first book called "Six Years A Friendship and A Baby" where I laid bare all the atrocities she had inflicted upon my husband and myself, this book you are reading now, purely focuses on the stalking part of what happened to me, publishing a book isn't for everyone I know, but it certainly helped me to shake my stalker and her band of vicious vipers for a while.

From June 2022 until June 2024, I had received thousands of messages of abuse, I was regularly receiving withheld number calls on my personal mobile and my work mobile, in this time frame my stalker had managed to discover absolutely everything about me, in fact she knew more about me than I knew about myself and it is still all ongoing today with no signs of stopping either.

When I published my first book, all stalking, abuse and harassment stopped dead, and for the week leading up to the book being published I had such a lovely break from the trauma of her silly harassment tactics, but I knew this would be a temporary thing and would not last for long, as my stalker had set a pattern of abuse that she had followed every day for so long now that it was now solidly ingrained in her and in her mind she just had to continue on, with her compulsive nature and obsessive personality I knew deep down inside that she was not going to stop, it had become a part of her life to terrorise and stalk others, it didn't matter who she was abusing as long as she was abusing someone.

A Woman Scorned Does Better Research Than the FBI

Over this two-year period, I had swiftly moved from denial to recording everything, after reporting all of what was happening to me to the police, 28 reference numbers and two police complaints later, I was already up to six A4 folders stuffed full of abuse.

It is all still happening but I have just stopped recording it all, I find it much more therapeutic to write books that help others instead (again, a little bit of English sarcasm here)

No matter what approach we tried nothing seemed to work and the whole toxic situation was just not moving forward at all, we had reached a stale mate and after we received yet another police email saying they were not intending to prosecute my stalker/harasser, that this matter was classed as a civil dispute between two parties, the police informed me that all our stalkers/harassers had been "severely spoken to" by the police, and I was advised to take out my own private prosecution, the last two lines of the email stated that the police were now closing our case and they apologised to us for not being able to prosecute my stalker.

Massive Sense of Humour Failure Alert!

This came as a huge disappointment to me, my friends and my family, not to mention my work colleagues who were all aware of what was happening to me, I was certain that the amount of evidence that was given to the police would be enough to gain a conviction, I personally found our case was not being taken seriously enough, and I was left feeling like I had no control over that at all, so instead of allowing this to drag me down further I sat down and started to write about my experiences with stalkers to help others manage the same kind of situation too.

If Life Gives You Lemons – Make
Lemonade – And Write a Book

Helpful Tip: get yourself a journal and write things down, it helps you to recognise patterns of behaviour, not only in your stalker but in yourself too. Start writing dates and times of what is happening to you, then in a different coloured pen underneath your description of the events that happened write a brief note on how it made you feel, I found this helped me a lot because I am a very visual person, I start to recognise patterns when I manage my data in certain ways, and me using different colours is one of those ways.

It became very clear very quickly what my stalker was trying to do, and by recording my data in a more organised way, it identified the methods she was using to attempt to get the reaction she wanted out of me and because I also wrote down how her actions were making me feel I could see that my emotions were being played on, this was psychological abuse.

By writing your own journal you will quickly be able to identify the sinister intentions of your stalker too, you will see patterns starting to form, you can identify how it is affecting you personally and how one emotion is being targeted by your stalker above all other emotions, this will allow you to target that unhealthy emotion with accuracy and precision this will allow you to manage a response tactic and work specifically in that one area so as not to allow yourself to be triggered into reacting, as this is exactly what your stalker wants.

The emotion my stalker was using to target me was identified as "fear" she was injecting fear into my mind, she was using specific tactics to control me using my fears of what "may" happen and not actually what has happened.

Gloves are off girly! I had discovered what she was doing and exactly how she was doing it too.

Take back the control.

CHAPTER FIVE

What is Stalking

The Definition of Stalking
We must take a look at what stalking actually is to be able to identify whether or not we are being stalked at all, so I have listed below the definition of stalking to help clarify things better:

Stalking is the wilful, malicious or repeated harassment or following of another person that would cause a reasonable person to feel alarmed or to suffer emotional distress. In general, stalking refers to repeated harassing and/or threatening behaviour by an individual.

This behaviour may include, but not limited to following a person; appearing at a person's home, school or place of business; making harassing phone calls; leaving written messages or objects; or vandalizing a person's property. Unwanted contact between two people that directly or indirectly communicates a threat or places the victim in fear can be considered stalking.

Source: The Law Regarding Stalking Current Through All 2001 Regular Session Acts. LA R.S. 14:40.2 Stalking.

Cyberstalking (also known as online harassment or electronic stalking) is the persistent offensive, threatening communication through the Internet, via e-mail, chat rooms or instant messaging or through other electronic means.

STALKER TRAITS

Stalkers are just not able to accept the work "no" they tend to display an obsessive personality and can display the following traits:

Jealousy

Narcissistic

Compulsive

Falls "instantly" in love

Manipulative

Does not take responsibility for own feelings or actions

Needs to have control over others

Socially awkward or uncomfortable

Views self as a victim of society, family and others

Unable to take "no" for an answer

Deceptive

Often switches between rage and "love"

Difficulty distinguishing between fantasy and reality

Sense of entitlement ("You owe me.")

Unable to cope with rejection

Dependent on others for sense of "self"

Views his or her problems as someone else's fault

May be of above average intelligence

Research reveals the typical female stalker tends to be single, in her mid-30s, divorced or separated, with a psychiatric diagnosis.

The most dangerous subgroup of female stalkers comprises those who stalk ex-sexual partners.

The most frequent motive behind a stalking campaign is the desire for a relationship—either to form one or rekindle a past relationship.

Regarding the nature of past relationships that lead to stalking behaviour, it is noted that in most cases where the stalker was an ex-partner involved a history of reported abuse.

On my husbands' medical records there is a note that clearly states: "being at risk from domestic abuse and emotional harm" this was added to his records while he was still living with his abusive exe girlfriend due to the ongoing verbal, emotional and psychological abuse being inflicted on him during their relationship.

It's reported that many stalkers do not change their behaviour at all, they merely change the object of their obsession, and this is exactly what happened to me.

My husbands' abuser became my stalker/harasser.

Therefore, trying to reason with a stalker is out of the question, they are delusional and do not respect anyone else' boundaries, they cannot accept that you do not want their unwanted contact and they will continue to stalk and harass you until something or someone else takes hold of their attention and they hopefully move away from you, I had to accept and deal with these facts, acceptance is key in moving yourself through such an awful experience, although you have no control on your stalker there are other things you can do to reclaim the control on your life and minimise the effect they have on you.

My stalker was fuelled by such rage, she held onto an unhealthy view of me and refused to let it go, she directed all her rage towards me daily and worked very hard at trying to destroy my life, my reputation and my sanity. She had permanent victim mentality and deflected the whole blame for her bad behaviour onto me, her warped sense of reality left her blaming me for the last 40 years of her life that I wasn't even present for! This is the kind of delusional person you are dealing with here and any attempts you make to reason with them in a logical mature manner are a total waste of your time.

I had never met this woman before, I had no connection to her directly or indirectly, no knowledge of her or her circle of friends and family, we didn't share any joint friends nor did we share any joint interests, and yet here she was making my life a total misery and all because I dared to date her ex-boyfriend long after their relationship had ended.

As I stated earlier, it was her refusal to accept that her relationship was over and that her exe boyfriend had moved on with his life led to her unhealthy belief that it was ok for her to stalk and harass me, she had told herself that I deserved such appalling treatment, and instead of accepting her part she played in dooming their relationship she found it much easier to deflect the blame onto my husband and me, this refusal to accept any responsibility and be accountable for her behaviour led to further stalking and harassment for me.

She had gone out of her way to find out my movements, the places I liked to visit, she discovered my place of work, I left my office one day to find her sitting in a layby 100 meters from the entrance to my car park, when I reported this to the police they said there was nothing they could do about her sitting outside my office, it is a public road and my stalker is permitted to park there, even though the police knew that what she was doing was attempting to intimidate me, it was clearly harassment and stalking, but I was informed that unless she was screaming at me or punching me in the face there wasn't a lot I could do about it because her just sitting there isn't breaking any laws.

The fact that my office is 30 miles away from my house is another matter altogether! It wasn't just a coincidence that my stalker happened to be outside my office on my dinner break, she had worked out my routine, what time I left for work in the mornings, where my work location was, what time my dinner break was and what time I left to go home again at the end of the day.

I came to realise that my stalker knew the parameters of the law and just how far she could bend them before she risked getting in trouble, it was like she had swallowed a book of the law whole!!! I found this absolutely infuriating, and little bit scary at the same time, but I never let her see that, I knew that if my stalker realised, she was upsetting me, she would just carry on doing what she was doing even more. I just had to tell myself that it was her effort, time and fuel she was wasting.

Everything my stalker did was an attempt to get me to overreact and lose my cool, but I am smart enough to know that if I lost my temper with her, she would twist things around and make me look like the bad person, so I refrained from ever hitting back at her and her flying monkeys that she had recruited in her hate campaign too. I adopted a method known as the "Grey Rock" you act like nothing happened and act all boring, so you don't give a stalker anything to gain their twisted pleasure from, I have to admit here that I really did struggle some days to not retaliate and hit back, I really had to work hard to remain calm, and most days my stalker never realised how lucky she was that I had good self-control.

It wasn't long before she realised that I was not going to react to her futile attempts in provoking me, from all the methods she had been using, from downright obvious to subtle and indirect attacks through other people and third party means, she knew the third-party tactics she was using were damn near impossible to prove, and she knew the police had neither the time nor the resources to investigate on a deeper level.

In the first year of being stalked the methods being used were mainly by use of mobile technology, I would receive emails, messages and phone calls, it later progressed to online cyber hatred, group mobbing and group hate campaigns, and the only way I had to defend myself was to keep blocking and deleting.

My stalker was using fear to intimidate me.

Fear runs deep inside us all, this is the biggest thing that holds most of us back in our lives, it blocks all other emotions out, our fears hold us stuck in one place, unable to move forward with anything, the person who manages to take hold of their fears and control them better gets to live a great life. You need to strike a balance with fear, too much and you become terrified of everything, too little and you are at risk of getting yourself into harms' way, but if you manage to have a better control over fear, you become so much more powerful in everything you do in life.

It is safe to say that at the start of my terror campaign I had no idea on how to deal with such a vindictive stalker, both my husband and me lived in constant fear of what my stalker was going to do next, but over time I began to see a way forward with it all, I began researching terror tactics and how emotionally weak people control more confident people, and it was surprising what I found too.

First thing you need to do is establish what kind of stalker you have, once I identified the type of stalker mine was I realised that I was able to start predicting her patterns of behaviour, so I began trialling my own ways to cope with what was happening to me and to attempt to move the situation forwards, it was at this point that I also came to the realisation that I wanted an end to what was happening but my stalker did not, here was me trying to find solutions and resolutions to put a stop to her stalking, but this was a pattern of abuse she had incorporated into her life and had been using for so long that she didn't want the drama to end, any of it, she wanted it to continue on, my stalker would probably not have anything worth while to fill the gap with in her empty life, and her stalking antics played such a large part in her life, she had gotten used to the excitement and drama that stalking provided for her, she had allowed it to be become a habit and like all habits, they become harder to break the longer we do them.

Types Of Stalkers Explained

The behaviour of your stalker totally depends on the type of stalker that they are, stalkers vary, some like to just observe their victims whiles others choose to project all their hatred towards their victims, my stalker was a rejected/resentful stalker, stalkers can be categorised into five main stalker types and I have listed them all below, you will find that stalkers fall into at least one if not a combination of two or more categories, once you have done a bit of investigating of your own on your stalker you should be able to profile them better:

The Rejected Stalker – stalking follows the end of a relationship

This isn't always the end of an intimate relationship, it can also be with estranged mothers, broken friendships and work colleagues, these types of stalkers are looking at either reconciling the relationship or exacting revenge. Most suffer from personality disorders and delusional disorders, they have the widest range of methods they use to stalk their victims, but mainly stick to harassing by phone.

The Intimacy Seeking Stalker – stalking based on their desire for intimacy

These stalkers identify with a person they see as their true love, they can be obsessional and delusional, due to suffering with a morbid infatuation of their targeted victims even if they are told there is no chance of ever having a relationship together, they will still maintain that they will be together eventually they also tend to be the most persistent in their efforts to stalk.

The Incompetent Stalker – stalking with a lack of social skills, stalker feels entitled to have a relationship with you

This group of stalkers tend to be known for stalking, they have stalked multiple people over their lifetimes, they become infatuated with their victims, but they lack the social skills needed to start a relationship and maintain it, regardless of these missing qualities they truly believe that eventually their victim will be with them, they target people they believe would make the ideal partner.

The Resentful Stalker – stalking meant to frighten victims

These stalkers intentions are to cause distress and frighten their victims, they act on perceived grievances against specific people, these victims are specifically choses and are most likely to be threatened by this kind of stalker.

The Predatory Stalker – stalking with the intent to sexually attack a victim

This type of stalker is the smallest group of stalkers and are made up of men only, they act in preparation to launch a sexual attack on a person and their behaviour makes them feel very powerful, they are very likely to have previous convictions for sexual offences.

Because my stalker had been rejected by my husband she didn't take this too well, she just could not accept their relationship had ended and she continued to pursue him, she fell into the rejected stalker combined with the intimacy stalker category right up until the point she discovered he had moved on with his life and met someone else, then she changed to a rejected resentful stalker, her traits overlapped and it made her advances towards me really uncomfortable and unpredictable, I only saw her as a threat once she tampered with the brakes on my car causing them to fail and she started taking my personal photos off my social media and using my information to threaten my husband with, she was attempting to terrorise us both, she wanted us to know that she knew what my name was and what I looked like, she also wanted to intimidate and frighten me into believing that she could get to me at any time no matter where I was.

As mentioned before, some stalkers like to just sit back and observe their targets but my stalker wanted me to know that she knew who I was and that she also knew what I looked like too. She was creating unwanted drama and attention, she wanted to inject fear into me, before she knew anything about me, she was using mainly voice, text, message and email to intimidate and terrorise my husband, she did try to get him to meet face to face with her, but he was too terrified of her to do this, she continued to threaten him saying she would hit him and hurt him, and the down side of them being in a relationship together for 6 years was that she knew all his routines, habits and his hobbies, she attempted to stay connected to him via his social network and his friends and family.

We got messaged by some of our friends saying she was asking about him trying to find out where he was visiting now, and once she discovered he was seeing someone else her efforts to gain intel on him doubled, she started trying to get herself invited to all the events she knew he attended, she tried "accidently" bumping into him in places she knew he visited, our lives became a living hell, we were watching for her everywhere we started going, if we had planned an evening out with friends we started going to places further away from our home, and we stopped posting our whereabouts on our social media accounts until a week after we had been there, we now had to second guess and counter act all her moves.

For the year leading up to our wedding we were not able to post anything on our social media for fear of her discovering our venue and crashing it, so we only posted things the year after our wedding had taken place. I couldn't share my excitement with any of my friends regarding my dress shopping or my hair and makeup trials, we took photos of it all and left all the photos in my phone ready to post exactly a year after we tied the knot.

When we went on our honeymoon, we never posted anything until after we arrived back home for fear of her breaking into our house while we were away, we now started living our lives way more mindfully, we had to think of every single eventuality, because we knew our stalker would.

Once your identity is known to a stalker, they are able to launch terror campaigns on you, they get to know your habits, your movements, they know the places your frequent and the friends you keep.

Every time we went out somewhere nice and posted on our social media we received fearful abuse in the way of spam emails, text messages, fake friend requests, direct messages on our social media from fake accounts. One tactic of my stalker was to direct message me using a fake account, once the message had been received into my inbox, she would immediately delete the fake account she had created, she knew that we would not be able to search it and take screen shots of it, we had to act really fast to report and block the accounts she was messaging from, but most of the time, the moment she sent a message she deactivated the account and we were not fast enough to report it and block it.

Her attitude was childish and immature, she seemed to get some kind of sick twisted kick out of directly messaging me knowing there was nothing I could do to prove it was her, this became a normal method of harassing me for her and her band of flying monkeys too.

Because neither of them worked they had all day to fire off all these silly things at us.

Acceptance: I cannot change how others behave towards me; I can only change how I react to them.

I had now reached a point that there was nowhere I could visit that my stalker didn't know about, within a year she had discovered just about everything there was to know about me, she even looked up my work contact details and started emailing spam into my work inbox, and my work mobile started to receive withheld number calls and silent calls the same as my personal mobile did too.

It got so bad that I had to request a new phone number from work, there was just no escaping from her.

Safety Tip: Get security cameras installed on your vehicles, get a good home alarm system because it really is a great deterrent and the footage you get is priceless, always have your mobile ready to take photos and videos every time you leave the house, and always be aware of your surroundings, and make a note of what is happening around you.

CHAPTER SIX

Why Do Women Stalk Other Women

We just reach a point with being stalked that we just need to know why this is happening to us in the first place, and we need to know what our stalkers are capable of doing, it is hard to believe that women are even capable of stalking or violence towards other women right?

Social stigma and expectations placed upon women are partly to blame, we think of women as the "gentler sex" all the descriptive words being used are softer and fluffier, we have been taught to see women as the home makers, the person who nurtures and raises the children, with natural mothering instincts that are inbuilt to love and encourage her family, not attributes of violence and hatred, women are not designed to fight and maim, this is why we struggle to identify with a woman who is capable of such awful behaviour, I am here to break that stigma and blow it wide open, cases of women stalking, harassing and abusing other women is actually higher than you think.

Our lives are getting harder with the cost of living crisis and the growing numbers of single parent families, women are finding themselves having to be a jack of all trades, they are not only raising the children and running the home, they are also having to work full time and pay all the bills too, the pressure on women is magnifying and when you squeeze a person so tightly they start to pressurise and explode in all different directions, women are made to feel like they are failing because they can't juggle so many things all at the same time.

We are all constantly bombarded with adverts and magazines depicting the perfect housewife, working mother and Goddess in the kitchen and bedroom, it's no wonder women are getting more aggressive, they are having to take on more of the male role of providing for their families as well as the female roles too, some women take to these challenges like a duck to water, while others don't cope with the pressure very well at all.

Having said this, nasty women is not a new concept, they have been out there in society all along, and it doesn't excuse bad behaviour in any way at all, it means we need to acknowledge that times are changing, women are having to constantly adjust and adapt quickly to the ever-increasing pressures being put upon them and we are now living in times whereby women's behaviours are becoming more aggressive all the time, and looking at the current trends, will continue to get worse over time too.

Mental Health disorders are increasing, and this plays a large part in female stalkers, I found that not only did my stalker have a mental health condition known as borderline personality disorder (BPD) but she also suffered with Narcissistic Personality Disorder (NPD) and mood disorder too, my stalker had also been diagnosed with depression, which would have been a symptom of her narcissistic personality disorder and mood disorder, now I am not a doctor and as such I cannot medically diagnose her conditions, but she had previously admitted being officially diagnosed to my husband when they were together, so I am safe in saying that she was suffering with these mental health conditions, the research that I was carrying out at the time of being stalked also confirmed stalking behaviours were more likely to be carried out by people suffering with a variety of mental health issues and one of those issues is BPD and NPD.

Coincidently my stalkers friend who she had also managed to convince to stalk and harass me too had openly admitted to suffering from borderline personality disorder, along with numerous other medical conditions such as depression, fibromyalgia, COPD from heavy smoking and many other conditions all self inflicted and too many to list, she had an addictive personality and found it easy to form new unhealthy habits really quickly.

So, it transpired that I had not one, but two stalkers who both happened to fit into the criteria of a female stalker, which I have listed below:

Female stalkers are mainly single, heterosexual, individuals in their mid-30s who pursue their victims for more than a year. They suffer with a majority of mental disorders and personality disorders, especially borderline personality disorder. They usually threaten violence and are more likely to be violent. Percentage of violence is around 25 percent, with limited use of weapons, likelihood of injuries is reported to be minor. Stalking victims were most likely to be male but can be female too; if the victim was a prior sexual partner of the female stalker, her risk of being violent toward him exceeded 50 percent. Unlike male stalkers who often pursue their victims to restore intimacy, these female stalkers often pursued their victims to establish intimacy and control. Common emotions and motivations included anger, obsessional thoughts, rage at abandonment, loneliness, dependency, jealousy, and perceived betrayal.

All the things that led to my husband being abused and stalked to begin with by his ex-girlfriend now led onto me being stalked and harassed daily, I remember thinking oh goody, I have a stalker when I was reading through research on the internet.

I laughed at this in the beginning, telling myself that I am the most boring person on the planet that she will soon get fed up reading or hearing about me! I kept telling myself that this kind of thing doesn't happen to ordinary people, that this only happens to celebrities and people whos' lives are in the spotlight.

I think I was like a rabbit caught in the headlights and in total denial for a while until I realised this just wasn't going away any time soon and I had to deal with it. I began researching the topic of stalking online, by the time I had got to this point we were about a year down the line. I had tried so many ways to get this to stop, had tried reasoning with them, had tried to appeal to them, had tried ignoring them, blocking them and reporting them, had taken them to court, and had them arrested three times in the space of 18 months but nothing was working. They just found other ways of stalking me and harassing me.

I really struggled to accept that this was other women doing this to me, my mindset was that nice people don't do this to other people, and the mistake I was making was allowing myself to think that these were nice people, when I could clearly see that they were nothing of the sort. Their lives were in a state of constant drama all caused by themselves, and the fallout from the trouble they made for themselves was all kept circling with no hopes of ever ending, they were creating unnecessary drama out of little to nothing and attempting to drag me into what is known as a triangulation drama.

As previously stated, neither my stalker nor her friend had many close personal friends, and I could see why too, no one

ME AND MY SHADOW

in their right mind would want to be their friends, they were loud, fowl and embarrassing, they were not able to hold onto friends for long periods of time, there was always some kind of big falling out which always led to a parting of the ways, they both suffered with antisocial tendencies and were socially awkward, their lives revolved entirely around what was happening inside their front rooms and any gossip they could pick up from people. This unhealthy attitude combined with them forever claiming to be the victim in any given situation was just adding to the drama they were creating. They shirked any responsibility and constantly blamed others for their bad behaviour, each time they contacted me, if I tried to talk sense with them, I was only ever met with unreasonable abuse and hostility, I gave up trying to reason with them and just blocked them instead.

Women who stalk and harass other women tend to have extremely low self-esteems, they are normally single in their mid to late 30s and have high levels of jealousy, you find their emotional level is very low and almost childlike, and their personal lives are totally lacking direction. They are social misfits, awkward in company, lack morals and do not have any respect for other people at all. Women who stalk tend to live in chaos, not only inside their own minds but they are not very good with finances or organising their lives, their homes are normally very messy and disorganised. They are totally lacking drive and ambition as the female stalker gets older her hatred for anyone doing better than herself increases.

When I was researching, I went online and put in the following search in the search bar "narcissistic personality disorder and stalking" and this is what it came up with:

"Manipulative behaviour: Narcissists are adept

65

> *at manipulating situations and people to meet*
> *their needs, often using stalking to intimidate*
> *others. Bullying: Fear and coercion are common*
> *narcissistic stalking tactics, stemming from a desire*
> *to assert dominance and control. 19Jan2024"*

I encourage you to do a bit of research of your own, you will discover so much, I gained so many helpful tips on what was happening to me and how I could try to stop it, although nothing I tried worked with getting my stalker to stop because she was hellbent on trying to control me with fear, her life was disorganised and she was working in total chaos, she was jealous and insecure, she hated me because I had the kind of lifestyle that she wanted but couldn't make happen for herself because she was too lazy to make it happen. She relied on the people around her to give her the things she wanted and to get things for her, she used other people as puppets to pay for things that she couldn't afford keeping the illusion she held in her mind that she lived a lavish lifestyle, the classic English saying of keeping up with the Jones' when she didn't live a rich lifestyle at all.

When we are younger, we all dream of who we want to be when we grow up, what we are going to be like as adults, our 16-year self may say, by the time I get to 25 I want to be settled down married with kids, or I want to become a successful businessman or woman and buy sports cars and fast jets! There are no limits to what you think you will achieve when you are a child, then as you grow older you get hit by expectations versus reality your visions start to take better shape, you start to realise what is important to you in life and what is not, and you start to make a plan on how you are going to achieve all the goals you set out to achieve all before you hit 30.

This is normal progression, we start off with a dream or vision of what we like, then as time goes by and we get older, we get influenced by other things that we want in our lives, and we start to learn to become flexible and adaptable, these skills are important in keeping you moving forward and not hitting a wall and becoming stagnant in your life, and having a flexible and adaptable mindset will always ensure you move forward and eventually get to where you want to be in life, when we experience failures in our ambitions and things that we had convinced ourselves that we really wanted to have, but never got them because we couldn't afford them at the time or we just missed timed things, we can always reason with ourselves in a mature understanding manner, we tell ourselves that we will have these things we want one day or we tell ourselves that it doesn't matter anyway as we have something much better, but with someone who is delusional and suffering with a personality disorder are not able to see the world with the same eyes as you and me, they don't hold the same beliefs as we do, their mindset is totally different to yours and their perspective is totally off.

Their egos are driving them on, it is all about the outside image they are projecting to the world, they convince themselves they deserve better in life, but they are not willing to work hard enough to get that, they rely on others to get things for them, their delusional state of mind refuses to allow them to see the reality of their situation and their inability to accept any blame on themselves also makes it impossible for them to see the error of their ways.

Female stalkers tend to be living with some kind of made-up fantasy life inside their minds, expectations that either they placed on themselves at an early age or others placed on them, within their own fantasy creation all of their own making they are the Queens and hold themselves in high regard above all others. When you first look at a female stalker you see an adult's body but they have a much lower emotional intelligence, and can be extremely childish in their conversations and interactions with others, it is no surprise that their lives are in total chaos, it is like having a beautiful house full of all the things you ever wanted and dropping an eight year old child in and expecting them to be able to run the household and pay all the bills without any issues, the female stalker does not possess the skills needed to organise her life, she is not able to focus on the things needed to have a happy successful life, she knows she is not able to do this and she is consumed with rage towards any other female who is organised and has their life in order.

If your stalker is known to you and you manage to catch a glimpse of what they look like you may be surprised. You have conjured up images inside your mind of a person who is impeccably dressed, with perfect hair and makeup, who has their whole life planned out in front of them and is so perfect that everything you do is some kind of annoyance to them right?

Wrong!

I had never laid eyes on my stalker, I had only ever seen photos of her that my husband showed me, photos of her at parties and social events appearing to be having fun, she was a rather large framed lady, but in these photos she was always dressed well and her hair and makeup looked lovely, she was smiling and gave off what seemed to be a good impression of herself in public, I had told myself that her life was in order and that she is organised to perfection and secretly named her Little Miss Polly Perfect, I imagined her house to be neat and tidy with, everything being sparkly clean, dinner being served on the table at a set time, and the whole household running like clockwork.

Expectation Vs Reality Check

I couldn't have been further from the truth, every way I had imagined my stalker to be was the total opposite of her. The first time I saw her was two years after her stalking of me had begun, I had gone back to my car in the car park after shopping in my local superstore, when I noticed her car parked meters away from mine, coincidently my stalker had parked her car in front of mine, for a moment I was frozen and I didn't know what to do, I was stuck rigid to the spot terrified to move my heart was beating so hard it felt like it would burst out of my chest.

I walked passed her car and headed back to mine, I quickly put my shopping away and just left the trolley by my car, I don't normally do that, I normally take the trolley back and put it with the others, but at this point in time I just wanted to hurry up and get in my car in case she came back and saw me, but what happened when I opened the door and got inside my car was strange, I just sat there frozen to my seat, I was struggling to control my breathing, my heart was still racing and my thoughts were all over the place, I started trying to calm myself down, as I knew I couldn't drive like this, I started to control and manage my fear, my breathing started to slow down and I found my thoughts again, the longer I sat there looking at her car the more I began to think of the things she would do when she returned to her car and saw me sitting there in my car a few feet away from hers.

I found I did the total opposite of what I wanted to do, what I wanted to do was drive away fast and get home to my safe place, but what I did instead was the total opposite, I decided to sit still and wait for her to come out and return to her car, I wanted to see if she started a scene when she came out of the store, I knew myself to be in the right, having arrived first and parked my car and she had arrived after, I knew she had intentionally parked near my car as an intimidation tactic, and I had reached a point where I was totally fed up with her childish antics, so I sat and waited, I was going to call her bluff!

While I was sitting there, I was running the last few years of her stalking campaign of threats and abuse through my mind, here I was sitting in the car about to test her to see if she would do anything to me at all, I felt like the lamb being led to its slaughter, I was having an argument with myself, asking myself why was I doing this? Why didn't I just go home? If anyone was looking at me, they must have thought I was really strange having these conversations with myself! And I must admit I was terrified, she was a very large woman and way bigger than me, and if I didn't shift quick enough, she could do me some serious damage.

My mind was wild with ideas of what she would do to me and how I could defend myself, my mouth was so dry I had to rip my tongue off the roof of my mouth, I was telling myself that I could do this, confront my stalker face to face, have it out with her, just get the whole thing over and done with and hopefully get to go home in one piece with no injuries to myself or my car, I wasn't too worried about myself as I taught ladies self-defence and judo years before so I knew I could handle myself in a prickly situation, it was the damage I thought she would inflict on my car, seeing as she had tampered with it previously resulting in having to have a whole new front end put on it.

So, I just sat there waiting for what seemed
like an eternity, time seemed to be moving
so slowly and then I saw her!

The shock of seeing her for the first time hit me really hard, she was nothing like how I had imagined her to be, nothing at all, in fact she was the total opposite, I thought she was taller, but she was in fact the same height as me a mere 5ft 2in, because she had injected so much fear into me, I imagined her to be giant sized, and the only giant size about her was her belly! If I said she was the same build as Father Christmas you would have an image in your head right, she was very large, she looked sad and lonely, she wore an oversized hoody that made her look even bigger, and she had horrible black sloppy jogging bottoms that were tucked into grey ankle length socks, wearing stripy black and white sliders, I looked at her totally stunned at what I was seeing, total disbelief at her appearance, surely this was not the same woman who had terrorised me so fiercely for over two years?

I had imagined her to be nicely dressed and really pretty but she wasn't at all, I noticed how dirty her car was and remembered my husband saying she never cleans it and it was always littered inside with lots of rubbish, she would take the dogs in there and never brush it out, her car was always filthy dirty and he never liked getting in it, plus her driving was horrendous, she drove dangerously fast everywhere without a care for her own safety or the safety of others.

I was in total disbelief at her appearance, I had pangs of sadness seeing her, she was not the person I had imagined at all, looking at her after never having seen her in the flesh before I began to realise why she hated me so much, I was everything she wasn't, I was living the happy life she only ever dreamed of, I had good friends, I went to nice places, and I made sure I had fun in my life, my family were lovely people and my children were successful.

After all that hype, after all that abuse and terror she put me through, here I was looking directly at her, I had my phone in my hand that I was ready to record in case she started something, I wanted factual proof of her terrorising me, but she didn't start anything, she didn't even look over towards me at all, and all I did was sit and watch her load her shopping into the back of her car without me moving at all.

I sat in disbelief at the sight of her, of how she was moving how her fat body looked, I just sat and watched her every move, I made a mental note of everything I saw, I saw the deep lines etched on her face, the black lines surrounding her eyes, her jowls that made her look unattractive, she had this saggy skin just hanging under her chin, how her face was twisted into a look of what can only be described as a bulldog licking piss off a thistle. I began to feel angry at this woman, one who had terrorised me and insulted my figure, my hair, my looks, when she looked like a sack of potatoes tied in the middle. She insulted my age when she too was an older woman! She had spent the last two years insulting just about everything about me that she could, and now I could see why she did what she did, and why she continued doing it too. She was insanely jealous of me, of how I looked, of how I dressed, of my life and all the things I do, she was deflecting all her failures onto me.

I was so angry at this woman, but most of all I was angry at myself for allowing her to intimidate and frighten me so much! And for so long too! What was I thinking! How did I not see any of this? How could I have been so stupid?

I could feel massive changes in my attitude happening inside my head the longer I sat there the more my mindset changed, suddenly it all became clear to me, she was delusional, she wanted my life, my friends, my family, she was stalking me to make comparisons between us, her life was in a total mess, she wasn't this slim attractive woman she had led me to think she was at all, she wasn't this popular person with lots of friends all going out for fun get togethers at all.

She was mean and horrible and fat and ugly, her personality was toxic, her manner was one of distain and jealousy towards everybody but herself, I waited until she had finished loading her shopping into her car and I watched her drive away, I continued to sit there for about 5 minutes afterwards just shaking and almost crying. I was so upset with myself for not seeing this sooner, for allowing myself to be hurt by her and her equally horrible friends, all of which were just as toxic as she was.

The time I had spent over the last few years trying to calm myself down and work on my pain and upset that she had caused me, I had become so obsessed with making notes that I had allowed it all to overtake my life and dampen my happiness, writing and documenting everything that my stalker and her friends were doing to me because I thought that somehow by documenting it all would prove to me and everyone else that I wasn't the crazy one here.

I held on to false hope that by documenting everything the police would prosecute them all and I would regain my freedom and happy existence that I had before all this started. But once I saw my stalker for real, I just stopped dead in my tracks! From that day onwards, I totally changed the way I thought about what was happening to me and how I reacted to it too, and even though I still get stalked and harassed via online cowardly methods today, I just take a quick screen shot and just leave it in a folder on my phone now. I refuse to give them anymore of my personal time, and on another positive note, my stalkers are giving me more material for future books!

I was left with all this anger inside of me that I didn't know what to do with, normally I would go walking or arrange a day out somewhere nice, but I was left feeling totally deflated like all the wind had been taken out of my sails, and I found that I just didn't want to do anything or go anywhere, I knew my mental health had taken a massive battering and I knew I needed to do something about fixing it.

This was a turning point for me

CHAPTER SEVEN

My Epiphany Moment

Where I had been recording and documenting everything for a period of three years, I had enough data to begin making a chart, I had already started doing this trying to stay one step ahead of my stalker anyway, and using my data that I had collected I was able to figure out the type of stalker she was, and that had helped me when I was standing my ground and facing her in the car park the day I saw her for the first time, I already knew what she was doing and why she was doing it, she saw me as a threat, and she was jeolous too, and the more research my stalker did on me, the more information she discovered about the kind of person I was the angrier she seemed to get and the more she targeted me.

I was being targeted for being a nice person!

After coming face to face with my stalker in my local supermarket car park and nothing happening at all, all the years of abuse and threats I had received from both her and her friend just lost all their power. I had allowed myself to think that something really serious would happen to me if we ever came face to face and once she had discovered all the places I visited she had started to visit them all too, again, making me think she was trying to bump into me on purpose and make it look like an accident, what kind of person does that? my reasoning came to the conclusion that she was looking for a confrontation with me, but the day we did "bump" into each other and nothing happened I realised I didn't need to fear her or any of her friends anymore, I changed that day and their hold on me had vanished.

After making a bar chart and listing headings for all the methods my stalker had been using to terrorise me, I started counting up all the times she had phoned me or messaged me and the results I got are listed below:

My Stalkers Most Used Methods To Be As Follows:

Text Messages
Phone Calls
Voice Clips (Got her friend to leave vile voice clips on my phone, she never did any herself, always used others to do this)
Emails
Driving by my house
Sitting outside my work
Vandalized our Christmas display outside our house (installed security system)
Constantly attempted to involve me in triangulation dramas with others
Gossiping to my friends
Relaying threats to me through other people
Third Party Contact (Getting other people to contact me, never her directly)
Dropped a tracker on my car
Vandalised my car/cut the brakes/constantly let my tires down
Sent unwanted items in the mail
Enrolled me in online sex sites/porn sites/dating sites/sex offenders' registers

Enrolled me for free online courses (easy because she didn't have to pay anything to register my details)

Enrolled me for spam emails (again it's all free to do this)

Applied for loans in my name

Attempted to hack my home network

Gained access to my personal emails (got one of her friends sacked for doing this)

Started driving on the roads I use to get to and from work (regularly had to change my routes)

Started shopping in my local store (that she had never shopped in before she knew I shopped in there, EVER)

The Emotions I Found To Be Driving Her Rage And Hissy Fits Were:

Anger and Hostility being top of her list

Rage at being abandoned by my husband

Narcissistic rage about everything, anything and nothing

Obsession

Loneliness

Jealousy

Retaliation/Revenge

Need for power and control

Projection of blame

Social Incompetence

Envy

Under the influence of alcohol/drugs

Humiliation and shame (her life was out of control and so were her eating habits and body)

I think in my stalkers own mind, they imagined themselves to be perfect in every way, they couldn't understand why my husband left them and why others eventually left them too, she imagined her life to be great and full of fun and laughter, when she was incapable of incorporating all these good things into her life in the first place. She held onto a firm belief that everything she did was right and that it was the fault of others around her that created these unwanted and unnecessary dramas, she verbally assaulted and physically attacked anyone who challenged her behaviour in any way at all. My stalker refused to take on board any opinion that did not align with her own.

Whether a stalker is known to a victim or not, there is one thing they all have in common, these women who stalk other women are all driven by jealousy and revenge, they see their victim as a threat to themselves, they take it upon themselves to start hate campaigns and smear campaigns upon their victims and actively encourage others to join in with them too, the more people a stalker and harasser can add to their campaign the more powerful and in control they feel, they work towards making the odds uneven so their victim has no chance of standing up to them, their terror campaigns are all designed to cause as much hurt and pain as they possibly can, and they will use any means available to them to get what they want too.

Some female stalkers work alone, they do all their stalking in secret as they don't want other people to know what they are doing, they know what they are doing is wrong and that other normal people would not support them in their efforts to terrorise innocent victims and this is the reason why they will stalk alone without letting anyone else know they are doing it, they are trying to maintain their false image of perfection to the outside world and also to themselves, the view others hold of them is the most important thing to them, and anyone who challenges their perfect external view of themselves with be ferociously attacked.

One of my stalkers was a classic example of this, she ran an online shop selling products, she had 4.5k followers on her page and she regularly posted about how great she was and how she supports charities and does a bit of fund raising, she would take photos of herself dressed various printed t-shirts with a charity name on it and post up a homemade video of her championing their cause, she posted up stories of how she is a single parent looking after all of her six children herself, she made herself out to be the victim in every situation, she regularly added descriptive posts on her social media pages specifically aimed at assassinating the character of anyone who opposed her at all in any way, it was discovered she had created more than a few different social media accounts too, one for her family and friends, several for the products she was selling and a few others for stalking and harassing people on.

When I reported her to the police, they investigated and it came to light that she had several accounts in her name all spelt forwards, backwards and using initials only, all created using different mobile numbers to register her accounts to, and the police were very interested in this piece of information.

After a visit from the police my second stalker deactivated three of her accounts and rewrote another, she changed her posts, took out derogatory remarks and reposted completely different posts altogether, what she failed to do was delete all the comments from her friends that still referenced the original post, plus, when you click on the three dots next to a post it displays the original post, the date and time it was posted and amended! So, all the evidence of her harassing others was still on her social media accounts all made "public" for all to see too!

Coincidently, my original stalker also did exactly the same thing too, she had used her social media to stalk and harass, when we reported her to the police all her accounts went offline, and she changed her mobile number to hide the fact that she had used it to harass both my husband and me with.

I found that my stalker and her friend had extremely low opinions of themselves, they feared getting older and their looks starting to fade, they knew that relying solely on their personalities to gain new friends and hold onto existing relationships would be a problem to them, and with both of them being of the cowardly nature, their hate campaigns mainly consisted of gossiping, spreading rumours, smear campaigns, text messaging, signing me up for spam emails and anything else that is free and untraceable, as you can see this was causing me maximum annoyance with little effort to both my stalkers, it meant they could cause me a lot of discomfort from anywhere in the country just by using mobile technology without even causing any disruption to their normal routines, they would wait until their kids had gone to school and then they were free to continue with their hate campaign and their normal daily routines with no witnesses whilst I was being forced into chaos. What made it even worse was they refused to change their lives for the better, what they did instead was try to bring me down to the same level as they were.

I felt like I had no one to talk to about my ongoing ordeal, my friends were ok to listen to me for a while but eventually they got bored of hearing about it all the time, it was taking over every conversation, I would frequently be met with a reply from friends of "Oh My God hasn't that stopped yet" but then no further offer to talk about it or get it off my chest.

I could understand why they didn't want to talk about it too, there was nothing they could do to help me at all, it was something that had just become a part of my life, everyone close to me knew about it, I never kept it quiet or hidden at all, that is the last thing you should do when you have a stalker, you need to let the people around you know about it, people around you can be extra vigilant and totally aware of the situation they may notice things that you don't and from a safety point of view, it means you have people looking out for you, your friends and family will most certainly get targeted by your stalker too, if your stalker is struggling to get any information out of you they will definitely turn to the people around you to attempt to gain the information they want to know.

Because the identity of my stalker was known to me and we lived in the same town, I found that if I was driving and I saw what I thought was her car or a car that was similar in colour or make and model to the car she drove, I would tense up. I wasn't frightened of her as such but more of what she would do.

Many times I challenged the way I was thinking and I began to recognise my feelings at the time, I would try to reframe my thinking and my feelings that I was generating, I was meditating more and listening to calming music in an attempt to get a grip of my emotions, and I began to suffer with high blood pressure during my time of being stalked, my blood pressure had always been on the low side all of my life, this was something I had never suffered with before, I also noticed that I began to experience constant headaches and blurred vision and after a quick visit to the doctor it was confirmed I was suffering with extremely high blood pressure issues, my doctor informed me that I had to work on getting my blood pressure down, I informed my doctor that I was being stalked and harassed and he told me that would contribute towards having this condition, he went on to explain that being in a constant state of stress can make you physically ill, and that you can experience a number of symptoms brought on by stress.

I knew my health was beginning to suffer as a direct result of me being continually stalked over a long period of time it had led to my body being in a constant state of stress, and I was now beginning to show signs both physically and mentally, once I started to write down everything that was happening to me and how it was making me feel I began to see the damage all the emotional and psychological trauma was having on me and I knew I had to do something about it and that I couldn't continue on like this any longer.

Signs And Symptoms Of Stress

Stress can affect us in many ways, our emotions, our body and how we behave. Sometimes when we are stressed, we might not see it to be begin with, and the danger comes when we just keep going without recognising the signs that our bodies are not coping very well.

I started to notice my frantically beating heart, racing thoughts, hyperactive personality and behaviours that all resulted from being massively and permanently stressed out and this was being caused by being stalked and harassed.

How stress can make you feel

If you are stressed, you might feel:

Irritable, angry, impatient or wound up.

Over-burdened or overwhelmed.

Anxious, nervous or afraid.

Like your thoughts are racing and you cant switch off.

Inable to enjoy yourself.

Depressed.

Uninterested in life.

Like you have lost your sense of humour.

A sense of dread.

Worried or tense

Neglected or lonely

Existing mental health issues getting worse.

Some people who go through severe stress may experience suicidal feelings. This can be very distressing. If you feel like this at all the helplines in England are:

*Samaritans helpline Call 116 123 or
email jo@samaritans.org*
NHS helpline Call 111 this is a 24 hours every day
SOS Silence of Suicide helpline Call 0808 115 1505
*Mind has some other contacts on their website
that you can email or call just don't suffer
alone, there really is no need for that.*

I never felt suicidal at all with my ordeal, but I do feel it is good to outline how it can make you feel and that there are people out there that care about you, you are not alone, there are people who are professionally trained in helping anyone who has suicidal thoughts, please don't leave it, if you feel you need extra help and support just reach out, these helplines are anonymous and no one will find out that you called them.

During difficult times it is very important that you build a good support network around you, if you are not able to approach any of your family members or your friends, then approaching your doctor is a good start, they can suggest other professional services that can help you, it is surprising the amount of support just one professional would be able to provide for you.

Aphysical Signs Of Stress

Hormones produced by our bodies cause many different physical effects, these might include some of the following:

Difficulty breathing

Panic attacks

Blurred eyesight or sore eyes

Sleep problems

Fatigue

Muscle aches and headaches

Chect pains and high blood pressure

Indigestion or heartburn

Constipation or diarrhoea

Feeling sick, dizzy or fainting

Suddent weight gain or weight loss

Developing rashes or itchy skin

Sweating

Changes to your periods or menstrual cycle

Existing physical health problems getting worse

If we experience high levels of stress, these physical effects can get worse. This can also happen if we experience stress for a long period of time.

In some cases, stress may cause more severe or long-term physical health problems. These might include:

Takotsubo cardiomyopathy (broken heart syndrome). This can feel like a heart attack.

The British Heart foundation has information about takotsubo cardiomyopathy.

Secondary amenorrhea, this is where you dont get your periods for three months or more. The NHS has information on stopped or missed periods.

I started waking up in the morning with what can only be described as massive headaches, and sometimes it was so painful it would wake me up in the middle of the night too, I would have a racing heart and be covered in sweat from head to toe, I had a feeling that something terrible was going to happen to me all the time and I just couldn't shake it off.

It began obvious that I wasn't handling the situation properly and if I am being totally honest here, I didn't know how to handle this situation, I had never experienced anything like it before, and despite me researching the topic, I still didn't know what to do to protect myself better.

I just found myself getting up every day and trying to make it to the end of the day with little to no dramas, I thought that by just ignoring what was happening that I would be ok, but I was wrong, I wasn't ok at all. I tried to tell myself that it didn't matter and that I was doing ok, but I was just kidding myself and once I stopped lying to myself and pretending everything was ok, that was the time when everything changed for me.

How stress can make you behave

If you feel stressed, it might make you:

Find it hard to make decisions.

Unable to concentrate.

Unable to remember things, or make your memory feel slower

than usual.

Constantly worry or have feelings of dread.

Snap at people.

Bite your nails.

Pick at or itch your skin.

Grind your teeth or clench your jaw.

Experience sexual problems, such as losing interest in sex or being unable to enjoy sex.

Eat too much or too little.

Smoke, use recreational drugs or drink alcohol more than you usually would.

Restless, like you cant sit still.

Cry or feel tearful.

Spend or shop too much.

Exercise less than you normally would or exercise too much.

Withdraw from people around you.

Some days it felt like the world was closing in on me, and I felt like I couldn't breathe, I just couldn't think straight either and the effort needed to do just the simplest of tasks was draining the life out of me.

Have you ever been made to feel like this? Are you currently being made to feel like this? Being stalked is going to make you feel totally helpless and will have a massive impact on both your physical and mental health, the longer the stalking continues the more at risk you are too.

It's important that you recognise these signs in yourself, listen to your gut feelings, only you know if you are managing your situation or not, you need to be brutally honest with yourself, and we all cope with a bad situation to begin with, and most times a bad situation resolves itself and goes away, then the process of putting it all behind you begins, but when it goes on for a long time, it starts to wear you down, so once you have identified that you are struggling you need to make a plan of action to help yourself.

CHAPTER EIGHT

Maintaining Your Personal Safety

I think one of the things that stays with me following my ordeal was the ability of my stalker to make me feel extremely unsafe when in reality I was much safer than I believed myself to be, all because she had acted so furiously and had subjected me to the most horrendous barrage of verbal abuse, she had threatened both myself and my husband, both directly and indirectly through other people and had made out that I was at risk of attack from her and her friends and family, this had left my mind racing in all different directions, looking back now I think it was the fear of the unknown that had led to me becoming so fearful of her and the thought of what she "may" do, instead of focusing on what she actually had done!

Narcissistic people are experts at controlling others through fear, they are well practised at it, my stalker had managed to control my husband for years through her outbreaks of uncontrollable rage, she threatened to carry out acts of violence without ever having actually carried any of her threats out at all, just the threat of something was more than enough to control him, and she knew that too.

The psychology she was using was that of the mother who always threatens to smack the child, but never actually smacks the child at all, the mother just delivers empty threats that she never carries out! The mother only needs to threaten that action to get the child to comply with what she is demanding it to do, the mother knows in her own mind that she has no intention of smacking the child, but the child doesn't know that, and so conforms without questioning the mothers need to control it, this kind of emotional coercive control that uses peoples fear is then allowed to become a regular pattern of behaviour as it is guaranteed to get the results the narcissist wants, and in absolutely every situation the narcissists has to win! They need total control over people.

My stalker was doing the same thing, she was spewing out terrifyingly worded threats that she knew were totally empty and had no intention of following through with at all, what she was saying to me was terrifying, but here is where all the power is......

*I DIDN'T KNOW THAT SHE HAD NO
INTENTION OF CARRYING OUT THE THREATS
SHE WAS MAKING TOWARDS ME*

How could I possibly know she had no intention to carry them out her threats at all, I had never met her before in my life, I didn't spend any time in her company, so she was free to say and do exactly as she pleased to terrify me.

She was relying on the fact that my husband was so scared of her, that for the first year that we got together he never left the house, only to go shopping or to go to work, he stopped attending all social gatherings and stopped going to all the places he loved going to for fear of coming face to face with her, my stalker knew that he would be telling me horror stories of how she behaved towards me, she was counting on him telling me how terrifying and scary she could be, and I kick myself now for allowing his fear of her to bleed into me and infect my healthy mindset.

Another tactic of a weak person, they project a false image of themselves onto others, when a terrifying account is relayed to other people indirectly by a third person it adds power to what is being said. The image created is one that is much bigger than the actual image itself, and a story is always better and more powerful and scary third or fourth hand, isn't it? When you hear someone talking of a terrifying person that everyone is afraid of, retelling stories of how they have managed to make everyone scared of them by being violent and aggressive, it makes you build up a natural fear inside of you without ever having to meet that person.

With a skilled narcissist they are always using mind games to control their victims and it took me a long time to figure all this out, in the beginning I was hanging off every word that was being screamed at us both, I was trying to be reasonable with people who were just totally unreasonable, they had personality disorders and at the time before I started my research, I had no idea what that entailed.

I just naively thought that once my stalker had the facts pointed out to her, that she would see reason and stop, but she didn't listen and the only version of the truth that she would accept was hers and no one else', even after the police and the courts were involved, and these are corporations that only deal with factual evidence, not with thoughts and feelings or personal warped perceptions on events, but with proven facts.

I think the frustrating thing for me was that no matter what I tried, no matter what approach I took, my stalker just continued on, there was no stopping her, no amount of trying to be sensible or reason with her was about to stop her behaviour, and this is what stalkers are like, they are head strong on their campaign to terrorise you, you have to accept you cannot convince them to stop, you cannot reason with them and you will never get them to see sense. I was totally wasting my time and effort trying to do so, but I didn't see this in the beginning, I was so wrapped up with trying to find solutions to help calm the situation and fix it.

Knowing this you have to ensure you put in measures to protect yourself from any threats made towards you or your family, first thing is tightening your online safety, then your circle of friends and family, then your personal safety, followed by the safety and protection of your home and your vehicles, if you haven't already put in safety measures then this is the perfect time to take a look at how to make your personal environment much safer.

If you have had a personal relationship with your stalker, then you need to revisit any joint accounts you may have held together, delete all joint accounts and make new ones, if your stalker like mine was not connected to you personally but was connected to your current partner then you have to safeguard your circle of friends, any joint friends will need to be spoken to regarding any unwanted contact attempts by your stalker, let people know what is happening to you, that way you have more people looking out for you and keeping you safe.

Log out of all active sessions on your social media, change all your passwords, start afresh with everything, set really strong unguessable passwords and revisit your security settings, shut down your privacy settings to friends only and remove all photos of yourself and family members off your profile pictures and background pictures, I put up cartoon pictures of me, nothing that could be used against me in any way at all.

Before I realised what information my stalker was gaining on me it was too late, she had already visited all my social media accounts and removed all photos of me, she now had a batch of approximately 80 personal photos! All of which she used to make fake accounts in my name using actual photos of me,

I felt so foolish. How could I have been so stupid? But then again, I had never had to live my life so carefully, my security was tighter than most, but on a plus note my stalker made me realise the many ways I was leaving myself wide open to further attacks by her and her friends and anyone else trawling the internet looking for victims, always turn the negative to a positive.

After revisiting all my security settings, I was able to lock down my personal information and withhold my details from her and others trolling my pages. Everything I posted was never marked as public it was always marked as "friends only" and I even removed the tag "friends of friends" as it meant that she only needed to get added onto one of my friends' social media accounts to see what I was posting, so by marking everything as friends only there was no way she could look at what I was posting unless she was added as a friend by me on my account, and never in a million years would I ever do that.

My stalker and her friends attempted for many years to get added to my social media accounts but they never succeeded, they stupidly used the same methods each time they tried to infiltrate my accounts, it was either fake accounts in hot looking women's names with numbers or letters after the false names, or names they used of my friends that they knew were on my accounts already, somehow they had found out some of my friends, but then again, some of your friends won't have tightened their security, so there is an opportunity to stalk their profiles if they are left open for all to see, the accounts attempting to get me to add them on my social media were brand new accounts minutes old with no information, no places no photos nothing on them and the first thing they did was send me a fake friend request, or ping me a direct message asking what I was doing that weekend or who I worked for!

Obvious or what?

However, I never did identify who it was that was sitting on my social media taking screen shots of my posts and sending them directly to my stalker! And I still do not know to this day, one of her many flying monkeys that she had managed to spin a convincing tale to, convincing them to report everything back to her as one of her personal little spies. I just made sure that anything I did post on my social media was with the knowledge that anyone could see the information and it was most likely going to be fed back to my stalker eventually. It didn't change anything for me at all, it just made me more aware of what information about myself was safe to post.

Don't include times and dates of places you visit either or places that you intend to visit at some point in time, and just handle all data about yourself as if it could lead to a kidnap attempt on you! Now I am not saying that you will be kidnapped, but I bet your stalker has thought about doing it a few times, in fairness I don't want to know anything that my stalker and her flying monkeys were thinking about, I don't think I want to have to attempt to process such nonsense and once you hold a terrifying thought in your mind that you didn't have before it is like planting a seed, it grows over time. So, no thank you, I am happy for them to keep all their thoughts all to themselves without me ever knowing!

The Advice We Received From The Police Was:

Keep all contact with the stalker or harasser to a minimum
Do talk to trusted family, friends, neighbours, colleagues or your manager about what's happening, if you feel comfortable doing so.
Trust your instincts and remember it is not your fault.

Report stalking or harassment to the police.

The police state that you don't need to collect evidence before you report stalking or harassment to them, but if you have already started recording events to do the following:

Record each incident as soon as possible afterwards and note the time and date.

Note details of any witnesses who may have seen or heard anything.

Keep a record of how the person harassing you looked: e.g. details of what they were wearing or their vehicle.

Keep messages or record any phone calls you receive.

Ask neighbours, friends and people you work with to record nay details if they witness anything.

Record it on your phone.

Staying Safe

Being stalked is not your fault, you didn't make a stalker stalk you or harass you that is entirely on them, you should never be made to feel as if you need to alter your life to keep yourself safe from harm, you should always consider the following to always ensure your safety:

Carrying a personal alarm.

Parking in well-lit areas or where there is CCTV installed.

If you are being followed, head for a place of safety.

Make sure your home is secure.

Secure all your Tech.

The Advice On Unwanted Calls Is:

If you don't know the caller, don't answer questions about

yourself, no matter how honest they sound.

If you have voicemail, don't include your name or number in the message.

A voicemail message should never tell people that you are out or away.

If you are listed in any directories, give your initials and surname rather than your full name.

Contact the police if you're being stalked or harassed, you have the right to feel safe in your own home and workplace. Stalking is illegal, but having said this, after three years of documenting everything and constantly reporting it all to the police, we applied to the British Courts for a Non-Molestation order with a Restraining Order with the Powers of Arrest, but my stalker and her friends constantly breached this order, and for us it wasn't worth applying for, despite reporting this several times to the police our stalker was never charged with breaching the order and eventually after another year of reporting everything we were told by the police that they would not prosecute my stalkers and harassers as it was seen as a public dispute between two parties and the police were not going to follow up with our case, we were advised to waste more money in taking out a private prosecution instead.

We both decided together that we were not going to continue to record what was happening to us any longer, it was taking up too much of our time, effort and monty to print it all off and file it all, however, on a plus note again, the three years of documenting everything gave us enough material to write our two books with the view of helping others who are suffering a similar experience to ours, we are trying to raise awareness of this ever-growing situation amongst members of the general public today and to offer help and advice to others going through the same thing as I did.

For the UK there is a National Stalking Helpline, every country will have their own support system for individual cases, and you will need to look up the country you reside in to obtain your, but the UK details are listed below for all the UK residents:

National Stalking Helpline
Telephone: 0808 802 0300
Monday – Friday 0930hrs to 1600hrs (except
Wednesday 0930hrs to 2000hrs)

The fact that there is a National Stalking Helpline at all tells me that this is an increasing issue, this has been recognised by someone who was kind enough to put in a helpline to help other people, how cool is that?

How do you move forward when you have suffered from being stalked, it's not just a case of taking your stalker to court to get them to leave you alone, the damage they have caused to you emotionally and psychologically will never go away, and you are not the same person that you used to be anymore, it makes you way more cautious, you suffer with being hyper vigilant in everything you do.

My cousin was also staked and harassed by her exe husbands second wife, they had been separated and divorced for over 5 years when she started receiving unknown phone calls, which then turned into unwanted contact.

We were out celebrating our first book being published, we had thrown an open invite to all our family and friends on our social media saying we were going to celebrate at one of our local pubs, lots of people came down to join in our celebrations, it was a lovely afternoon with full sunshine, and my cousin had told me that her exe husbands' new wife had taken it upon herself to launch a hate campaign against her for absolutely no reason whatsoever other than the fact that this woman was jealous of her. This woman was jealous of the fact that my cousin had married her husband before her, luckily there were no children involved and when the marriage ended, they both went their own separate ways with no further contact being made between them, absolutely nothing for 5 years, until........

It was some 5 years after this that my cousin began receiving horrible calls and messages from her exe husband's new wife, it started with name calling, and empty threats and then led onto continued harassment and smear campaigns, it followed the same pattern as my stalkers smear campaign and harassment too, and this seems to be the normal pattern for all stalkers and harassers!

My cousin managed to get hold of her exe husbands mobile number and called him while his new wife was stood next to him, she admitted everything and told him it was because she was jealous of her, she did promise that she would stop and my cousin received an apology from both her exe husband and his new wife for the trauma that had been caused, but it didn't stop there, it never does, the stalking and harassment continued on.

My cousin told me of a time that her and her new partner were out trekking somewhere and bought one of those lovers locks that you snap onto a bridge somewhere pretty, she said it was a lovely little padlock in the shape of a frog, they snapped it onto the bridge took a photo and then posted the photo she had taken on her social media, the next day a dead frog was delivered to her home address, it had been sent through the post. My cousin told me that we all knew who it was, but what can you do about this kind of thing? The police just class it as a one-off incident with no real evidence of the person you claim to have sent it admitting to sending it, you can't provide any witnesses, so you are left with no other choice but to carry on and await the next childish act.

My cousin is a wonderful lady, she doesn't deserve this kind of treatment, she is kind and funny, very attractive and people naturally gravitate towards her warm bubbly personality, the conversation is easy with her, and you find this great sense of ease just chatting together, she would never hurt anyone.

I have always loved my little cousin deeply, I used to babysit for her and her brothers when they were younger and I was privileged to watch her grow up into the lovely young lady that she is today, and when she first told me that she had also been stalked and harassed for many years, I got very angry. How dare this woman who my cousin had never met before be so cruel to her, and I found myself wanting to protect her.

We talked some more and my cousin told me she too had tried all the things that I had been doing to protect myself and that there was nothing further she could do about getting the woman to stop either, so we both sat talking about how we deal with this kind of trauma, how being out of control makes you feel, and that we are in no way responsible for any of what is happening to us.

The normal "sticks and stones may break my bones" thing just doesn't work in situations like this, you feel totally helpless. You keep asking yourself "why me! What did I do to deserve this" and the answer is, you didn't do anything to deserve this, in fact everything that is happening to you is nothing to do with you at all, it is all to do with the stalker, my cousin and me sat chatting about our experiences and it was a comfort to see that we were saying exactly the same things to each other, we didn't do anything to make these women stalk us, and there is absolutely nothing we can do to make them stop either, we have to sit and hold onto hope that our stalkers eventually get bored of us and move onto fresh targets and leave us alone.

We talked about how every time we did something nice or fun that it always got back to our stalkers, and they took great delight in trying to ruin our day by being nasty in some way. Their jealousy drove them insane knowing we were enjoying our lives, and they were not.

My cousin was delighted that I was writing books to spread encouragement to other women on how to manage such an awful thing, she even offered to tell me some stories to include in them too, I may make a miniseries of personal stories by other women.

I have concluded that if you are pretty, have good manners, you are happy and fun to be with, you have a good life and great people to share it with then you are going to get stalked by another woman at some point in your life. You need to take it as a compliment really.

Stalkers don't target ugly ducklings you know; they target the beautiful swans.

Carry on being the beautiful swan that you are, keep forging forwards in your lives, keep being that lovely person that you know you already are.

END NOTE

Moving Forward

Whilst I was researching I came across a website that was packed full of positive quotes and I liked them enough to share them with you, I have included them in my book to help anyone who needs a little mental lift, some of these quotes we have heard many times before and some not so much, my favourite is "What doesn't kill you, makes you stronger" and "While they are picking on me they are leaving someone else alone" I find these are quite powerful quotes, we all endure suffering in our lives, the important thing is how you manage yourself through it all, and one thing I love to do is help others who are also suffering too.

You may have a few favourites of your own that inspire you, and it would benefit you greatly to highlight the quotes that help you the most, write them out and dot them around your house to keep reminding you of the great person you are, I have inspirational quotes on my desk in my office at home where I like to sit and write. I find it really helps me to slip into a better mindset, it enhances not only my wellbeing and my thoughts but also impacts on my performance too. I am just an ordinary person, that has experienced extra ordinary events in my life and am now trying to share my experience with others in order to help them to move through this chaos we call life.

40 Encouraging Quotes To Share With A Friend Who Needs Help

Words have the power to liberate, heal and comfort when given to a friend in need at the right time. Even if you are not physically together, you can show your support by sending them words of affirmation and encouragement when they go through tough times. If you're unsure about what to say to unburden a friend in need, maybe you shouldn't say anything at all. In some instances, friends greatly appreciate random gestures such as an email or a text message.

At the end of the day, it's always the thought that counts.

Encouraging Quotes

"We do learn something about ourselves when we are up against the wall, and we do most certainly come out stronger." – Tina Sloan

"Humans are creatures of habit. If you quit when things get tough, it gets that much easier to quit the next time. One the other hand, if you force yourself to push through it, the grit begins to grow in you." – Travis Bradberry

"Sometimes when you are in a dark place you think you have been buried, but actually you have been planted." – Christine Caine

"In the middle of difficulty lies opportunity." – Albert Einstein

"Believe you can and you're halfway there." – Theodore Roosevelt

"Embrace uncertainty. Some of the most beautiful chapters in our lives won't have a title until much later." – Bob Goff

"Whenever you find yourself doubting how far you can go, just remember how far you have come." – Unknown

"No matter the number of times you fail you must be determined to succeed. You must not lose hope. Don't stop in your storm." – Tony Narams

"Soon, when all is well, you're going to look back on this period of your life and be so glad that you never gave up." – Brittany Burgunder

"Without failure there is no achievement." – John Maxwell

"For any problem, no matter how big or complex it may be, there is a solution." – Earl Nightingale

"Through difficult experiences, life sometimes becomes more meaningful." – Dalai Lama

"When you lose everything, you get depressed if you don't step back and start appreciating what you do have." – Paul and Tracey McManus

"Every day may not be a good day, but there is good in every day." – Unknown

"Just remember, there are no quick fixes. But, by taking action just a little bit every day, you will build up a powerful reservoir of confidence, self-esteem and discipline." – Scott Allan

"Relentless people move mountains. Relentless people make the impossible, possible. Relentless people achieve miracles." – Wayne Allyn Root

"I may not be where I want to be, but thank God I am not where I used to be." – Joyce Meyer

"If you accept other people's negativity, you allow your life to be limited by their lack of imagination." – Nick Maley

"You will not always be strong, but you can always be brave." – Beau Taplin

"When things go wrong, don't go with them." – Elvis Presley

"Never let your past decisions determine your future outcome." – Mark Dudley

"Yes, I know some days are more difficult than others. But if you program your mind in a positive way, you won't have to drag through certain days just hoping to get to Friday so you can finally enjoy life." – Joel Osteen

"The greatest test of courage on earth is to bear defeat without losing heart." – Robert Greene

"Never blame anyone in your life. Good people give you happiness. Bad people give you experience. Worst people give you a lesson. And the best people give you memories." – Zig Ziglar

"Although the world is full of suffering, it is also full of the overcoming of it." – Helen Keller

"The will of God will not take us where the grace of God cannot sustain us." – Billy Graham

"Nobody deserves your tears, but whoever deserves them will not make you cry." – Gabriel Garcia Marquez

"Remember your dreams and fight for them. You must know what you want from life. There is just one thing that makes your dream become impossible: the fear of failure." – Paulo Coelho

"The scariest moment is always just before you start." – Stephen King

"Great things never came from comfort zones." – Neil Strauss

"Never let the odds keep you from doing what you know in your heart you were meant to do." – H. Jackson Brown Jr.

"Never confuse a single defeat with a single defeat." – F. Scott Fitzgerald

"Ever tried. Ever failed. No matter. Try again. Fail again. Fail better." – Samuel Beckett

"Don't let what you cannot do interfere with what you can do." – John Wooden

"That which does not kills us makes us stronger." – Friedrich Nietzsche

"Your mind is a powerful thing. When you fill it with positive thoughts, your life will start to change." – Unknown

"Your big opportunity may be right where you are now." – Napoleon Hill

"Life begins on the other side of despair." – Jean-Paul Sartre

"Once we believe in ourselves, we can risk curiosity, wonder, spontaneous delight, or any experience that reveals the human spirit." – E.E. Cummings

"If you take risks and face your fate with dignity, there is nothing you can do that makes you small; if you don't take risks, there is nothing you can do that makes you grand, nothing." – Nassim Nicholas Taleb

Take Action

If you find the quotes above highly helpful, take the time to share it with a friend who would appreciate them greatly.

You may not realize it fully, but sometimes redemption and comfort can also be found in meaningful words.

It may not mean much to you at first glance, but to others, the message may just be the very thing that they need to hear.

Make a difference in the life of a friend and forward these encouraging quotes today.

Credit given to Tomas Laurinavicius April 29, 2024

DO NOT OVERRATE WHAT YOU HAVE RECEIVED

NOR ENVY OTHERS

HE WHO ENVIES OTHERS

DOES NOT OBTAIN PEACE OF MIND

BUDDHA

REFERENCES

DynaTAC 800x invented by Martin Cooper working for Motorola in 1983

National Association of Child Contact Centres (NACCC)

Child Support Agency (CSA)

Samaritans Helpline: 116 123 and email jo@samaritans.org

NHS Helpline: 111 its open 24/7

SOS Silence of Suicide Helpline 0808 115 1505

The Charity Mind

National Stalking Helpline: 0808 802 0300

The Law Regarding Stalking Current Through All 2001 Regular Session Acts. LA R.S. 14:40.2 Stalking.

Tomas Laurinavicius April 29, 2024 for inspiring quotes

These telephone numbers may change so it is best to do a fresh search on the internet if you intend to make contact with any of the above.

ALSO BY KIMBERLEY ALICE

Six Years A Friendship and A Baby: Surviving and Thriving after Enduring Emotional and Psychological Trauma.

Printed in Great Britain
by Amazon